Beyond the STORM

Finding
God's
Calm
Assurance

Beyond the STORM

DR. JERRY JONES

HOWARD
PUBLISHING CO.
West Monroe, Louisiana

Our purpose at Howard Publishing is to:

- *Increase faith* in the hearts of growing Christians
- *Inspire holiness* in the lives of believers
- *Instill hope* in the hearts of struggling people everywhere

Because He's coming again!

Beyond the Storm
© 1997 by Howard Publishing Co., Inc.
All rights reserved. Printed in the United States of America

Published by Howard Publishing Co., Inc.,
3117 North 7th Street, West Monroe, LA 71291-2227

Second printing 1998

Library of Congress Cataloging-in-Publication Data
Jones, Jerry, 1938–
    Beyond the storm : finding God's calm assurance / Jerry Jones.
        p. cm.
    ISBN 1-878990-71-3 (alk. paper)
    1. Consolation. 2. Encouragement—Religious aspects—Christianity. 3. Hope—Religious aspects—Christianity. 4. Faith. 5. Despair—Religious aspects—Christianity. 6. Loss (Psychology)—Religious aspects—Christianity. I. Title.
BV4905.2.J654 1997
248.8'6—dc21   97–7902
                                                                          CIP

Jacket Design by LinDee Loveland
Edited by Philis Boultinghouse

"More Than Conquerors" © 1978 Birdwing Music BMG Songs, Inc. & Mighty Wind Music. Admin. by EMI Christian Music Publishing. Used by permission.

Scripture quotations not otherwise marked are from the New International Version, © 1973, 1978, 1984 by International Bible Society. Used by permission Zondervan Bible Publishers.

All italics in Scripture were added by the author for emphasis.

DEDICATION

Very seldom does an author connect the dedication of the book to the contents. However, the dedication of this book is different. Many individuals have walked with me through the storms of my life, but two have been constant.

The first is the wife of my late brother. She has always been more of a sister than a sister-in-law. She is a woman of great strength, courage, and determination. She is known as a lover of people and an unequaled caregiver. Her counsel is wise and her heart is big. Thank you, Flo Jones Rowland, for forty plus years of friendship.

The second is a partner in the gospel. I first met this person in 1966, when she was working as a secretary and I as a young Bible professor. Her secretarial skills are unmatched, and more importantly, she has the courage of her convictions. As a friend she faithfully serves behind the scenes without fanfare or recognition. Her quiet walk with God is respected by all. Her serving heart is constant and consistent. Thank you, Peggie Baker, for thirty years of work, service, and friendship.

I have never thanked these two women enough for their support through the years. It is my prayer that this dedication will communicate what I have not been able to say. I am reminded of a statement about the women in the ministry of Jesus:

> Some women were watching from a distance. Among them were Mary Magdalene, Mary the mother of James the younger and of Joses, and Salome. In Galilee these women had followed him and cared for his needs. (Mark 15:40–41)

Thank you Flo and Peggie.

C O N T E N T S

PART ONE
Voices from the Storm

PART TWO
Assurances from God's Word

How to Read This Book

This book has two parts.

The first part—"Voices from the Storm"—is a collection of testimonies from men and women who have felt the pelting rain and the fierce winds of the storm, who have been swept up in the powerful currents of rising waters and have finally made their way to the shore and found peace once again. Each story is written from the heart, even though recalling the pain still hurts. The storm victims who share these stories have been honest with their feelings, so if some of their feelings seem negative, that's because storms bring negative things into our lives.

The testimonies are arranged under four categories—death, terror, divorce, and illness. While there are many other categories that could be included, the principles shared in these stories apply to storms of all kinds. Not only do these storm victims tell their own personal stories, but many tell what they have learned and provide helpful insight into survival and recovery.

The first chapter shares stories from those who have suffered the loss of a loved one—my own story included. Death strikes the young and old, the weak and the strong. Few of those left behind are ready for the adjustments that are demanded. Life must go on, but it's never the same. Family reunions, holidays and special events offer painful reminders of the emptiness that can never be filled.

Chapter two contains stories from victims who survived some horrific terror. Victims of a catastropic accident, a rape, and a murder share their stories and how they survived the storm.

The third set of stories are from those who have survived the storm of divorce. Divorce brings demands and problems unlike any other storm of life. Rejection, hurt, verbal and physical abuse, and broken promises make lasting and deep scars. The loss of the dream can be nearly unbearable. No one really wins, regardless of who is declared guilty or innocent. While death brings finality, divorce carries lifetime regrets. "What if?" can be replayed time and time again. The physical presence of an ex-mate is a reminder of what should have been, but for some reason is not to be.

Chapter four shares the stories of three families who struggled with serious illness over many years. Personal long-term illness or that of a loved one creates financial problems and physical burdens on others. The pull between quantity of life versus quality of life becomes very real; an irreversible illness may trigger troubling reevaluations of hard-and-fast convictions. Not knowing how loved ones will be provided for in the future drains emotional energy. Being dependent on others doesn't appeal to anyone.

Very seldom does any one person's storm parallel another's, but there are many common denominators. Although storms vary in intensity and type, each storm is "big" to the one experiencing it. Some of the most difficult storms to face are those that are not of our own making and that no amount of "fixing" can change.

Part 2 of this book is my answer to those who have asked how I have been able to handle the storms of my life. When the storms of life devastate your world, you want more than the assurances of a preacher or author or friend; you want to hear from God himself. This section asks four of the "big" questions that haunt storm victims—"Is God really with me?" "Does God really care?" "Is there life beyond this one?" and "Why must we suffer?"—and then provides "Assurances from God's Word" that can be counted on.

Even though you might not relate to the specifics of each story in Part 1, you will find gems of wisdom and insights into survival in each story. The biblical assurances of Part 2 are words that you can truly depend on, for they are based on the Word of God.

This book isn't a cure-all for every storm you could ever face, but it is a beacon in the night declaring that you *can* make it through the rough waters and the storming seas. While in the pit of the storm, we need to believe that we can make it to the shore. This book will provide evidence that others have walked in your shoes and have reached the peaceful shore. It will encourage you to read of others who have walked through the fire and have emerged without smelling like smoke. As one who cried out, "I want my life back to normal," I soon learned that the testing of lives by storms *is* normal.

This book is written to reassure all those who are in the midst of storms that there is a brighter day in the future. As you read about the scars of fellow travelers and learn how God helped them to heal, you can be assured of your healing as you continue walking in the minefields of life.

The question isn't whether storms will come, but when, where, and how often. This book is written with the hope and prayer that it will sustain you through your storms and enable you to someday guide others through theirs.

INTRODUCTION

> A furious squall came up, and the waves broke over the
> boat, so that it was nearly swamped. Jesus was in the
> stern, sleeping on a cushion. The disciples woke him
> and said to him, "Teacher, don't you care if we drown?"
> (Mark 4:37–38)

Have you ever felt like these disciples? Your life was progress-
ing nicely—the sun was shining, the winds were calm, the water
smooth—then all of a sudden, a furious squall comes up and the
waves break over you, and you are nearly swamped. Gasping for
breath, you are knocked off your feet—so stunned that you

hardly know what hit you. And you look up to heaven and you say, "Don't you see what's going on down here? Don't you see that I'm about to be swept out to sea and drowned? Don't you care?"

That's how storms are. They take us by surprise. They knock us off our feet. They wrench the breath from our lungs. They fill our hearts with doubts and fears. They turn our eyes to heaven in search of help—and sometimes we can't see the help, and sometimes we don't know if we're heard.

This book is written by and for storm travelers. This book is about surviving the storm.

This book is also about the end of the story we began on the previous page. When the disciples went to Jesus and asked for help, this is what happened:

> He got up, rebuked the wind and said to the waves, "Quiet! Be still!" Then the wind died down and it was completely calm. (Mark 4:39)

If you've experienced a storm, you've yearned for what Jesus brought to the whirling winds and tossing sea—complete calm. He provided it for them, and he'll provide it for you.

Most of us grew up with the perception that right always wins over wrong—that the good guys are rewarded and the bad guys are punished. As small children, the stories of *The Three Little Pigs* and *Cinderella* reinforced these perceptions. As we grew older, we watched *Superman, Top Gun,* and *Star Wars.* Good and evil may have struggled during the course of the story, but when the show was over—the good guys had won and the bad guys had been punished; the innocent were freed and evil was exposed.

But then we experienced the reality of life, and our dream world began to fall away. In real life, we saw the innocent punished instead of rewarded; we saw evil win and good lose. And because right and truth don't always win, struggles set in.

For most of my early life, I saw good things happen to good people. I grew up in a loving family where I received encouragement from my parents and enjoyed a close relationship with my brother.

My high school experience was filled with sports, parties, and dating. During college I studied, played sports, made friends, and received honors. I met a lovely Christian lady and married her during my senior year. I reared three children in a strong, Christian atmosphere in a small town in Arkansas. I eventually completed a doctor's degree and assumed the position of chairman of the Bible Department at a small Christian college, with the rank of professor. My reputation as a speaker grew to the point that I was frequently invited to speak to large audiences.

Everything was going great, and life's challenges were minimal. I envisioned living my whole life in that small town and retiring from teaching at the college with a forty-year pin.

However, the next eleven years brought a lifetime of storms. In May 1983 my whole family felt the blast of the storm when my twenty-eight-year-old nephew was killed in a race car in full view of his father and brother, leaving a wife and small baby. The very next week, my own personal world was blown apart when I was dismissed from my job of seventeen years for what I considered unfair and unjust reasons. In 1984 I moved my family to the Northeast to work with a church. This move traumatized my family. Because of some serious conflicts of beliefs, I disassociated myself from this movement in 1987 and became a man without a church. That very same year, my mother died.

In November 1989, the storm accelerated its force into a full blown hurricane when my wife of thirty years was diagnosed with malignant lymphoma cancer of the spine. The days, weeks, and months of the next five years were defined by hospitals, doctors' offices, and chemo and radiation treatments. When I thought the waters could rise no higher, in September 1993, I was engulfed in sorrow when my only brother died suddenly at age sixty-two of a ruptured aorta. Then, just forty-five days later, a very close friend of twenty-three years died while on a flight from Houston to London, England. Two months later, another good friend died while playing basketball. At the same time, we were told that my wife had only a few months to live. (She actually lived another year and died a very painful death on November 10, 1994.)

During all of this trauma, I tried to keep my sanity and to be a rock for my wife, my three children, and my friends. It seemed there would be no end to the hurt that I saw on every front. It seemed the storms would never cease and the challenges to my faith would never stop.

I had never turned my back on God and his Word, so I began to search and pray like never before. I don't remember ever being angry at God during this time, but I do remember some awfully loud conversations with him.

As I began to share with others what God and his Word were teaching me, I saw the need to write this book. I have written eleven other books, but this was the first book to find me. Most of my books have been the result of academic research; this one is the result of a search for answers to life's struggles. When I realized that storms are the common lot of all people, I decided to plot my journey for the benefit of others. There is no way I would have sought the experience necessary to write this book—hence, I say, this book found me.

As difficult as life's struggles are, I have learned that there are benefits in struggle. The struggle the caterpillar endures as it emerges from its cocoon strengthens its wings and allows it to fly. Without struggle, the butterfly would not be able to fly. We do the caterpillar no favor by helping it out of the cocoon. So with us. Our struggles develop our spiritual muscles and enable us to "soar on wings like eagles" (Isa. 40:31). As you read the stories of the men and women in this book, you will see a recurring theme. No one prompted the storytellers to write of this, but so many did. Over and over you'll hear: I never would have chosen to go through this storm, but now that I'm beyond it and see all the blessings I've gained and the lessons I've learned, I wouldn't trade the experience for anything.

I've also learned that the most essential ingredient to surviving the storm and its aftermath is *faith*. Scripture tells us that "we live by *faith*, not by sight" (2 Cor. 5:7). Without faith, enduring trials is impossible. And if our faith is to sustain us through the storm, it must be our own. It must be a faith of choice. We cannot ride out a storm on the faith of others.

But Jesus does not ask us to take a "blind leap" into faith. Faith in Jesus is built upon a reliable historical record. You don't have to hook on to the faith of someone else; you can examine the facts for yourself and come to your own conclusion. When you accept the fact of who Jesus is—the Son of God—you accept his statements as true, and Jesus' teachings become trustworthy because of who he is.

Jesus asks each of us the question he asked Martha, the sister of Lazarus.

> Jesus said to her, "I am the resurrection and the life. He who believes in me will live, even though he dies; and whoever lives and believes in me will never die. *Do you believe this?*" (John 11:25–26)

Do you believe this? Do you believe that Jesus is the resurrection and the life? Do you believe that he can resurrect your broken life and provide real hope for the future? Your belief in Christ is the foundation that enables you to survive the storm.

In the gospel of Matthew, Jesus told a story about storms and how to survive them.

> Everyone who hears these words of mine and puts them into practice is like a wise man who built his house on the rock. The rain came down, the streams rose, and the winds blew and beat against that house; yet it did not fall, because it had its foundation on the rock. But everyone who hears these words of mine and does not put them into practice is like a foolish man who built his house on sand. The rain came down, the streams rose, and the winds blew and beat against that house, and it fell with a great crash. (Matt. 7:24–27)

Whether or not we endure the storm depends on the foundation of our house. If we practice the words of Jesus and put our faith in him, we will still be standing after the storm has passed. When the storms of life beat upon your house, Jesus' truths will hold you together.

My wife, Claudette, was in the hospital for sixty-two consecutive days in 1990. She was in intensive care for thirty-five days and on a respirator for twenty-five of those days. Her faith and trust in God helped her (and many others) through this ordeal before she succumbed to death on November 10, 1994. People often remarked that her faith must have developed during those sixty-two days. But she always declared that her faith was developed *before* this ordeal; she said she was too sick, too tired, and too weak to build or develop her faith during those stormy days. Faith must be intact before the struggle comes, because it isn't easy to develop faith in the middle of a storm.

While a personal faith doesn't guarantee that you will *understand* the storms of life or survive the storms in the way that *you* plan, it will give you the confidence and strength to survive.

Have you ever read the end of a thriller before you read the story? When you know how the story ends, you don't feel the same tension while reading it—you know that everything turns out okay. Or have you ever watched a taped version of an important athletic contest after you knew the ending score. You were able to watch the game without the emotional trauma of a live viewing because you knew the outcome. Being behind in the second, third, or even fourth quarter produced no anxiety because you knew the outcome. Reading the book of Revelation reveals the outcome of our own personal storms, and the good news is that the outcome of your Christian faith is *victory!* Knowing this doesn't take away the pain and weariness produced by the storm, but it will help you *endure* the storm.

My brother taught me something that has greatly shaped the way I've viewed the storms that have passed over me. He refused to call his struggles "problems," but viewed them simply as *challenges.* When the storms come, we have very few choices but to face them. It is up to us to view them as either stepping stones or stumbling blocks.

Perhaps this easy-to-remember poem will remind you of God's constant love and care.

> Yesterday God helped me.
> Today he'll do the same.
> How long will this continue?
> Forever—praise his name!
>
> (source unknown)

PART ONE

Voices

Voices from the Storm

CHAPTER 1

Voices from the Storm of **Death**

INTRODUCTION

Very few make plans to die. And very few plan for the death of their loved ones.

For those left behind life is never the same. The vacant spot at the dining table, the unoccupied living room chair, the half-empty bed, the painful void at family gatherings and special holidays—the death of those we love affects us for the rest of our lives. As unsettling as the subject of death is, the Scriptures are clear about its reality.

> Man is destined to die once, and after that to face judgment. (Heb. 9:27)

Why, you do not even know what will happen tomorrow. What is your life? You are a mist that appears for a little while and then vanishes. (James 4:14)

All men are like grass,
    and all their glory is like the flowers of the field;
the grass withers and the flowers fall,
    but the word of the Lord stands forever.
(1 Pet. 1:24–25)

The first story in this chapter is my own. The death of my precious life-mate, Claudette DuBois Jones, was the inspiration for this book. The struggles I faced, the strength the Lord provided, the blessings of family and friends, the hope for a continued life, the courage to go on—this is what I share with you in my story, and this is what the other storytellers in this book share through theirs.

In Memory of *Claudette*

Claudette taught me much about living but even more about dying.

When Claudette and I married in December 1959, I never dreamed she would precede me in death. She began her five-year battle with cancer in November 1989 and died in November 1994.

Claudette's illness began with simple back pain. After many visits to the doctor, cancer was discovered in her spinal column between her shoulder blades. During the next five years, she received radiation and chemo treatments. While she had brief periods of remission, the cancer always resurfaced in other areas of her body, and it was always inoperable.

On October 3, 1992, Claudette's birthday, the doctors told her she wouldn't live to see her next birthday. Claudette wrote an inspiring article titled "My Last Birthday," which appeared in the

Christian Woman magazine. Claudette did live to see her birthday in 1993 and in 1994, but because of her gradual decline, she eventually required supplemental oxygen, a wheelchair, and constant care.

When Claudette realized that the treatments were only buying her time and were never going to cure her, she began to prepare herself, me, and the rest of the family for her death. She kept a journal of her thoughts. She boxed up items she wanted each child to have. She made last visits to friends, relatives, and her mother. She discussed her funeral plans in detail with me and told me what to do with the family the first Christmas without her.

Claudette taught me much about living but even more about dying.

In spite of pain and the pressures of her illness, Claudette maintained a positive and cheerful attitude. She had few periods of depression. In fact, those who visited her left feeling blessed by her. Claudette had the ability to see humor in serious situations. Two situations I will always remember. One of the side effects of the morphine she was taking for pain was uncontrollable jerking—she would drop books or pencils or even slap herself accidentally. On a routine visit, a nurse asked, "Claudette, how are you doing with 'the jerks'?"

Claudette said, "I'm doing just fine; I've gotten used to them."

"How did you get used to 'the jerks'?" the nurse asked.

Without missing a beat, Claudette said, "I've been living with one for thirty-five years!"

The second situation occurred in connection with her medication. One morning she sat down near me in the family room and asked me to dial a number on the telephone as she picked up the receiver. I didn't know who I was dialing, but after a minute I realized that she was talking to the Wal-Mart pharmacy. She told the pharmacist that she needed to have a prescription refilled and noted that the prescription was for a sixty-day supply, and then she said, "I am a terminal cancer patient; so I only need a thirty-day supply." When she hung up the phone, I was at a loss for words. How should I respond? I finally said, "I imagine you wouldn't buy green bananas, either!"

The last week of Claudette's life was difficult. Because she chose to die at home, we had to rent a hospital bed for her. She objected to the bed because she saw it as a step down in her recovery, even though she knew she was dying. Two of my three children, as well as several close friends, were present when she died. When death and relief finally came for her, the atmosphere in the house was joyful; we all knew that Claudette was now free from pain and that she had won the victory.

Seeing one you love slowly die over a period of five years isn't easy. I know. Losing a loved one in an accidental death is hard, and losing a loved one due to unexpected health problems is likewise difficult. Each type of death carries with it a different set of emotions. Recovering from the death of a loved one is a very individual matter. There is no right way or wrong way to handle death and grief. Even though no two situations are ever the same,

I believe that the following lessons I learned along my journey can bless the lives of others.

View death as a reality for all people. Despite the precautions we take, we can't control how death will come. Death brings pain; pain is the price we pay for love. If you didn't love so deeply, the pain of loss wouldn't be so great. Expressing grief is natural. Paul declared that he would have had "sorrow upon sorrow" had Epaphroditus died (Phil. 2:27).

Bring closure to the death of your loved one. In my case, I had the assurance that I had done everything I could to sustain Claudette's life and make it comfortable. We had time to reaffirm our love and appreciation for one another. Once she was gone, I needed to close that chapter of my life. However, some don't have the opportunity to say and do all they can for the deceased, and this can result in guilt. The one left behind to grieve must accept the fact that no situation is ever handled perfectly and that doing it differently might not have been better than the way it was done. There's nothing more you can do for the loved one who died; you must go on with your life.

Learn to deal with the newfound freedom one day at a time. I had been married for thirty-five years, and it felt strange to be single. I had become free in a new way. The admonition to live one day at a time is the best available. Trying to project months down the road isn't wise.

Develop close relationships with others. Have these relationships in place before and after the death of a spouse. You need some sounding boards for your thoughts and feelings. Choose those who will be open and honest with you and who may, at times, disagree with you.

Do something for yourself. If you have been a caregiver for a long time, you need to invest in yourself a little. I'm not suggesting that you buy a new red sports car, but a shopping spree might be in order, as well as some short trips with friends.

Translate your loved one from the present to memories. Accept the reality that your loved one isn't coming back. You will always have memories to cherish, but you will never have his or her physical presence again. Death isn't the extinguishing of a light; rather, it is the turning off of a lamp because the dawn has come.

Death isn't the extinguishing of a light; rather, it is the turning off of a lamp because the dawn has come.

Learn to live life among problems. Sometimes problems are a result of our actions, but many times, they come through no fault of our own. Life has never been problem free. You may declare the unfairness of life, but this too is a reality of living.

You can be a better person as a result of living through adversity. When others face the same challenges you have faced, you can speak with credibility. You have a deeper empathy for others. Your ability to minister to others will be enhanced.

Trust in the Lord's wisdom—anyway. Adversity demands a trust in God previously unknown. The answer to *Why?* can be forever unanswered. Failure to see good in adversity is common, especially when there is no rhyme or reason for it, but you must trust anyway. It isn't easy to walk by faith and not by sight.

Creating a new agenda for your life isn't wrong. There can be more than one plan for your life, and finding a new direction can be exciting and challenging. Choose to bloom where you have been planted. The roads of bitterness and self-pity bring unhappiness and depression. You may feel limited in your ability to go on with life, but going on will ultimately bring the greatest sense of accomplishment and happiness.

—Jerry Jones

In Memory of *Mike*

Nightmares sometimes come true. Unspeakable fears sometimes become reality. It happened to Job. It's happened to some of you. And it happened to me.

January 23, 1988, I gave birth to my firstborn son in a small town in western New York. Four miscarriages and thirty-four years had preceded little baby Bradley's arrival. In pleading with God for a child, I had bargained away my body parts. "Please, Lord," I would pray, "I'd give my right arm to have just one child." But every month came the answer: *no.*

The odds were strongly against me. Scar tissue from the miscarriages had left me with 75 percent blockage in my fallopian tubes. A myomectomy (surgical removal of fibroid tumors) three years earlier, no pregnancy in the following three years, and my own thirty-three years of age further reduced my chances for a baby. Hope was fading fast.

When I discovered I was pregnant again, no one was more shocked than I. All of my previous pregnancies had ended in miscarriage by the end of the third month, so we began cautiously watching the calendar, afraid of hoping again, afraid of hurting again.

The beginning of the second trimester came, and we were still in the game. Was it too much to hope for? Maybe. But we couldn't contain our excitement. The next six months passed quickly. And I didn't even have to give up my arm! To me, it was truly a miracle.

As I waited in my room the morning after my son's birth, a nurse came in, walked over to my roommate, sat beside her on the bed, and put her arm around her. They exchanged a few quiet words, the nurse placed her baby in the bassinet, and the three quietly left. Odd, I thought.

A few minutes passed. I heard footsteps coming. I recognized my nurse as she came into my room and felt disappointed that she didn't have my baby. Two steps behind her was my mother-in-law, immediately followed by my father-in-law, immediately followed by a sheriff.

I heard alarms. Alarms so loud in my head I could barely hear anything else—but there was a woman somewhere screaming.

My nurse touched my arm. I felt her hand shaking, saw the tears in her eyes. No sound came from her mouth, but I could see her lips say my name.

My mother-in-law came to the other side of my bed. She also touched my arm. She leaned down and whispered in my ear, "There was a fire."

I heard that woman screaming again, and she was saying, "Mike is gone!" And then I realized that the woman I heard was me! My husband was dead.

"What I feared has come upon me; what I dreaded has happened to me" (Job 3:25). It's been seven years since my husband died. I remember it as if it were yesterday. It feels like yesterday. It sounds like yesterday. The tears are as hot on my face today as they were January 24, 1988.

I heard alarms so loud in my head I could barely hear anything else.

How does a young woman survive the death of her husband? Who helps her put the shattered pieces of her life back together? How does she rebuild a home alone? Who can she lean on until she can stand alone? Where does she begin?

I carried my grief like an eggshell in my pocket, protected, yet so fragile. I lost control of my life. I was afraid, confused, and alone. I had lost the one who would share all the joys and pains of my son's new life.

The road through grief isn't an easy one. It often must be traveled alone. One night I fell deeply into that pit called grief. I called my dearest friend to come be with me. Picking up the phone to ask for that kind of help was hard for me. I was the invincible woman, or so I thought. I was strong. I could do anything. But this night, I was afraid. I was alone. I could do nothing.

And she couldn't come. I felt she had abandoned me. I felt she had chosen not to come. (I was wrong to feel that way.) It was to be one of my longest nights. "Save me, O God! The water is already up to my neck! I am sinking in deep mud. There is nothing to stand on. I am in deep water. A flood is sweeping me away. I am exhausted from crying for help" (Ps. 69:1–3 GOD'S WORD TRANS-LATION).

That night I felt panicked. Terrified. My mind was filled with fragmented pictures. Darkness. A man alone. A house filling with heat and smoke. A man crawling, dragging across the floor. Calling out to me. Flames surrounding him. Sirens. Flashing red lights. Men. Lots of them. Calling his name. Calling my name. Looking for us. Giving up. Daylight. Digging through hot ashes. Looking for charred bodies. It was as if I could see myself in a corner of the room. My back was to the wall. There was no place for me to go. "Oh God!" I cried. I cried the same words over and over and over. I slid to the floor, unable to move. I don't know how long I sat there, but in my aloneness, I began to feel another presence. A friend was by my side. I was comforted by the one who also was once alone. He knew my pain. He knew my confusion. He knew my fears. I felt his warmth, his strength. I knew that I had never really been alone. My Savior had been my strength. He had held me up when I couldn't stand, and carried me when I couldn't walk. And when I was ready, he would stand back and walk beside me. I would find life after death.

Sin had been in control of my life. Was Mike's death my punishment? No. God loved me and wanted me to come home. He opened the door and held out his arms to me. I ran to him, hungry for his loving, gentle arms to surround me with comfort that no one else could supply.

I was unable to pray with words. But I was sure that the Holy Spirit was able to understand my groanings and my tears and to express them to my heavenly Father. I looked to him for strength, wisdom, and guidance for this enormous task of building a new life and raising my son alone. I searched the Scriptures daily for words of comfort and direction.

> Do not be afraid, because I have reclaimed you. I have called you by name; you are mine. When you go through the sea, I am with you. When you go through the rivers, they will not sweep you away. When you walk through the fire, you will not be burned, and the flames will not harm you. I am the Lord your God, the Holy One of Israel, your Savior. . . . Since you are precious to me, you are honored and I love you. I will exchange others for you. . . . Do not be afraid because I am with you. (Isa. 43:1–5 GWT)

I began regaining control of my life. Someone once said that when God closes a door, he opens a window. I still had a lot to learn about doors and windows. I still had a lot to learn about who should control my life.

Nineteen months after Mike's death, I felt I had accomplished the task of creating a new life for my son and me. I was involved in the business of living. Then the time arrived: I went on a date. I was sixteen and sixty-six at the same time. It was wonderful! I had missed male companionship. I no longer felt guilty for thinking or saying it. I was not the one who had died. I was alive! And it felt good!

Still, something was missing. And I knew what it was. I packed our things, and Bradley and I moved six hundred miles to my hometown. I needed to be near God's people. I needed to be near my old church family, my physical family, those who knew my sins and my failings and loved me anyway. I needed to change the direction of my life. It isn't enough to just stop doing the things you should never have done in the first place. So I surrounded myself with God's people. I was learning who was in control of my life. He opened the window, and I opened myself to his direction. I had lost control, I had taken control, and now I was yielding control. I was a different person. I had learned how to survive life's tragedies; and I had learned where to turn for strength.

I had lost control, I had taken control, and now I was yielding control.

Our Lord is very kind to me. Through his kindness he brought me to faith and gave me the love that Christ Jesus shows people. This is a statement that can be trusted and deserves acceptance: Christ Jesus came into the world to save sinners, and I am the foremost sinner. However, I was treated with mercy so that Christ Jesus could use me, the foremost sinner, to demonstrate his patience. This patience serves as an example for those who would believe in him and live forever. (1 Tim. 1:14–16 GWT)

When you allow God to control your life, get ready, because things happen! I received a phone call one night from a man I slightly knew. Phil was a member of our church. He taught our Wednesday night adult class; he was a nice guy and was going through a divorce. I guessed he was about five years older than I and far too serious about everything. (Divorce can do that to a person.) He asked me to accompany him to see Hal Holbrook perform as Mark Twain. The timing was incredible. It was on the second anniversary of Mike's death. But I didn't hesitate. I said I would love to go. (I didn't even mind being his second—or was I his third?—choice!) I looked forward to an evening out and to being in his company.

When he came to pick me up he was bearing a gift for my two-year-old son, Bradley. If it's true that the way to a man's heart is through his stomach, then it must also be true that the way to a woman's heart is through her children.

We enjoyed the performance and about a gallon of coffee afterwards. There was never a lag in conversation. I learned he was actually three years younger than I. His enjoyment for living had been buried under the weight of his divorce. We seemed to have many things in common and enjoyed each other's company. I liked him a lot, and I felt I had found a new friend. We closed up the restaurant after midnight.

Within a few short weeks, we began to feel that someone else was in control of our relationship. We felt drawn to each other. We seemed to share ideas on just about everything. We talked on the phone into the wee hours of the night, and then found it difficult to function during the day on just a few hours of sleep—like teenagers, only with less energy. Neither of us was looking for anything more than friendship and companionship. But it wasn't long before the "M" word was mentioned. We felt this was what God had planned for us all along. I was not afraid. God was in control of my life. And so on March 10, 1990, we made a lifetime commitment to each other.

I am full of peace with my life today. My second miracle child, Caitlin, was born on October 25, 1991. Eight weeks later my husband became a full-time minister, fulfilling his lifelong dream. My son has a daddy who loves, protects, teaches, and plays with him. I am whole.

Does it still hurt? Yes. It will always hurt. But I choose to place my grief in its proper place and go forward with my life.

Not long after my husband's death, I received a phone call from a staff member of the hospital where I had delivered my son. She remembered the circumstances that had surrounded my son's birth—that my husband had died an untimely and traumatic death. There was a young woman from a nearby town with a two-week-old baby daughter. She had multiple sclerosis. Her husband had just died in a snow skiing accident—another nightmare come true. She would be going home from the hospital soon, and she was having a very difficult time. "Can you help her?" the nurse asked. I told the nurse to give her my phone number. I wanted to help her. I would try my best. After all, isn't that what 2 Corinthians 1:3–7 is all about?

> Praise be to the God and Father of our Lord Jesus Christ, the Father of compassion and the God of all comfort, who comforts us in all our troubles, so that we can comfort those in any trouble with the comfort we ourselves have received from God. For just as the sufferings of Christ flow over into our lives, so also through Christ our comfort overflows. If we are distressed, it is for your comfort and salvation; if we are comforted, it is for your comfort, which produces in you patient endurance of the same sufferings we suffer. And our hope for you is firm, because we know that just as you share in our sufferings, so also you share in our comfort. (GWT)

That is what I do. I share my pain so that you may know you are not alone. You can survive. There is one who is always there for you to lean on—24 hours a day, 7 days a week, 365 days a year, your entire lifetime—no matter what. I know.

As I write this, I am waiting for the results of a biopsy done on my uterus. Pretty scary. But I know that *I am okay* with whatever the future holds for me because I know who has *always* held my hand. He held my hand in February 1977 after the first miscarriage; on April Fool's Day, 1977, when the motorcycle on which I was the passenger was broadsided (I was in the palm of his hand on that one! Not only did I kiss death, but the accident caused my second miscarriage). He was with me in 1983 when I was broadsided again (broken ribs, punctured lung—relatively minor stuff). He helped me survive two more miscarriages in 1983 and 1984 and a life-threatening staph infection in my bloodstream in January 1985. And, finally, he never left my side through the entire year of 1988 after my husband died. Why should I be worried about a biopsy? He never lets go. We do.

I live my life now for God, but I haven't forgotten who I was. I still can't believe that he selected me to live a life in his service. Can you? I am who I am because he loves me—because he has always loved me. I can do anything because he strengthens me.

Are you dealing with the death of a spouse? What can you do?

- *Want to heal!* Pray for healing. Believe he will heal.

- *Bear your pain.* Grief is not a bottomless pit! It only feels that way.

- *Learn about the* process *of grief.* Understanding the process removes some of your fears.

- *Allow grief to run its natural course.* You can run, but you can't hide.

- *Talk about it.* Sharing aids the healing process.

- *Allow yourself no more than ten minutes of pity each day.* Then do something for someone else.

- *When others ask how you are, don't say "fine" unless you are.* And if you do when you aren't, don't complain when you feel abandoned.

- *Give yourself time.* Healing takes place at a different pace for everyone. Do your own time. Grief can't be rushed.

- *Don't make any major changes* in your life for the first year unless absolutely necessary.

- *Expect life to change.* Learn to be alone. Set new goals. Choose to make a new life for yourself. Choose to like yourself.

- *Do the best you can,* then let go of it. Don't look back.

Allow yourself no more than ten minutes of pity each day.

The widow's walk is frightening and lonely at times. But it is only a walk, not the end of the road. My Savior wants to be your Savior. He never lets go.

P. S. The biopsy was normal. See? I told you!

—Vicki Cox

IN MEMORY OF *Rob*

When my husband died of a spinal injury in a racing accident at the young age of twenty-seven, my life ended—at least I thought it had.

I was twenty-four years old, with a one-year-old daughter and not a clue as to what was in my future. How would I cope? How would I survive? How could I be both mother and father? At that time in my life, Rob's strength was my strength. How could I ever be strong without him? These and many other questions went through my mind, and I had no answers for them. I was all by myself, and I didn't know if I could make it.

Rob and I met in 1971. Our relationship actually began due to my friendship with Brenda, Rob's little sister. Brenda and I met when I visited the church she attended. Brenda and I became very close, and, to this day, we have a friendship that I treasure.

Rob and I started dating in 1975. He took me to a drag race on our first date. Where else would a racing enthusiast take a date? From the beginning, I learned that racing was an important part of Rob's life. And it didn't take long for me to realize that it would play a major role in our future.

I was twenty-four years old, with a one-year-old daughter and not a clue as to what was in my future.

As Rob and I spent more time together, I found myself being accepted into his family as one of their own, like a daughter. His family, like my own, was full of love and close-knit, but they added a spiritual element that I found genuine and inviting. Three years after our first date, in March 1978, Rob and I were married. Now, I really was a member of the family.

Our life together was probably pretty typical of most young married couples. The only difference may have been that Rob was a successful builder and driver of race cars in the Midwest racing scene. It wasn't too long after we were married that he had a garage built in our backyard so he could concentrate on his car-building skills. Rob felt this was an advantage, and, indeed, he was very respected among his racing companions because of his expertise. But more importantly to Rob, the new garage enabled him to be closer to his family and to spend more time with us.

Shortly after the garage was completed, I learned that I was expecting. Rhonda Gail was born in May 1982 and quickly became her daddy's pride and joy. We seemed to have it all—the love and support of our families, good health, a prospering business, and a successful racing career. Life was going well.

In March 1983, Rob and I celebrated our fifth anniversary. It was very special to us because of all the family and friends who celebrated with us. Less than two months later, we celebrated our daughter's first birthday. Rhonda had actually been due in early June. But the fact that she was born early gave Rob the opportunity to celebrate her first birthday, for twenty days later, he was gone. I have been ever grateful that Rob was able to celebrate this special day.

Rob's death caused me a great deal of pain. As a young, widowed, single mother, I suffered various emotions: anxiety, loneliness, inadequacy, and anger. I was angry at God and at Rob. Why did Rob have to live his life on the edge? Did he not consider the dangers? Did he not consider the pain he could cause? Didn't he care if we were left alone? Again and again I would cry out, "Why did you do this? How could you do this? Do you know how hard this is?" Did he not know how his death would affect those who loved him? It wasn't fair for us to have to endure so much pain.

I was angry at God and at Rob.

I had asked Rob not to go that night. He had just recovered from a serious illness that required several days in the hospital, followed by two weeks of overtime work at his shop. I just wanted him to spend time with us. Besides, his car wasn't ready. He was only going with his dad and brother to watch. Our last conversation was a disagreement over whether or not he should go. I wish it could have been different. If I had known that it was to have been our last time together, I would have made it different.

That night was the worst night of my life. Had it not been for so many close family members and friends, I'm not sure how I would have managed. I am especially grateful to my mother who didn't leave my side until I finally fell asleep from exhaustion. She was truly a blessing. It was the best expression of her love that she had to offer.

The days that followed were filled with grief and pain. As I look back, I now know that they were also the beginning of recovery. Hundreds came to offer sympathy and support. The line went on and on at the funeral, and I was overwhelmed with gratitude toward everyone who wanted to share our pain. They will never know how much their supportive presence meant to us that day.

As the healing process began, I wasn't sure which road I needed to take. But one place I had to go was to the track where Rob had died. It wasn't easy, but I wanted to let his racing fans know how much I appreciated their support for Rhonda and me. I spoke to the crowd, and during my address, I thanked them; but I also spoke of the uncertainties in life and how we all need to be prepared. That was a difficult but necessary step toward closing that chapter of my life.

My spiritual journey since this tragedy hasn't always been smooth. In fact, life has been hard, and I have often asked God why this had to happen; but I have finally been able to accept the fact that I may never have a definite answer.

During this difficult time in my life, I gained strength from three primary sources. First, I found strength in knowing that

God continued to work in my life. I felt overwhelmed with trying to live, but I knew God understood my pain and would help me through it. God was patient and loving, and as time passed I found myself getting to know him in a deeper, more meaningful way. Now he is a close, personal friend. I read John 16:33, which opened my eyes to the idea that God would never abandon me. Listen to what God told the apostles. "I have told you these things, so that in me you may have peace. In this world you will have trouble. But take heart! I have overcome the world." If we could all learn this, I am confident we would handle trouble better. I strongly recommend staying in the Word and allowing God to reshape you in his own time.

Second, I found strength in other caring individuals who allowed me to release my pain in their presence. Specifically, I was able to share with Rob's parents because they had experienced a loss equal to mine.

Third, this chapter would be incomplete if I didn't mention how important my current husband, Jim, has been in my life.

Jim and I had known each other for years. Interestingly, he was Rob's childhood friend. They grew up in the same congregation, and I knew Jim throughout my relationship with Rob. About a year before Rob's death, Jim enlisted in the Air Force. After spending three years away from home, he returned and we started a friendly dialogue. We started dating and were eventually married on February 1, 1986.

Jim has been a wonderful husband and a good father to my daughter Rhonda. In September 1990, God blessed us with a son whom we named Jimmy. In addition to Jim's being a great husband and father, he has also been a supportive spiritual partner. He has strongly encouraged my spiritual pursuits, and he currently serves as a deacon and leads our youth at church. His involvement with our congregation has played a vital role in our family. His loyal support has been significant in my journey back to spiritual health.

Life sometimes is a series of crises. God is the solution to them all, and faith is the path that leads to God, who helps us handle our problems. God has promised that "to everything there is a season." The sooner we understand this, the better off we will be in handling life.

I don't understand why this had to happen, but I do know that God is fully capable of blessing our lives if we are obedient and allow him to. Thank you God for being there.

—Jan Williams

In Memory of *William and Ray*

My first husband, William Bottom, was electrocuted in 1958 while working for Texas Light and Power Company in Hillsboro, Texas.

I was pregnant with our third child when my mother and a Texas Power and Light official brought me the unwelcome news. I was completely devastated. I had no direction, no goals, and no employable skills. I was angry and bitter, knowing that preventable adverse work circumstances had facilitated my husband's death. Friends and family rallied around me and my children, and we moved in with my own widowed mother. My brother quit college to come home and help us. In retrospect, I can see that I was depressed, resting mainly on the faith of my mother. I lacked spontaneity, was unable to share in the joys of others, and certainly was unable to make effective plans for the future. Ultimately, recognizing that I needed employable skills, I attended a business school where structure and focus returned to my life.

I met my second husband, Ray Evans, when he became associate minister of the church I attended. Ray had two dreams: one was to be a missionary and the second was to teach in a school of ministry. While Ray was in the master's program at a Christian university, we learned of a missionary program in the Netherlands. After graduation, we gathered support and left for the Netherlands with our four children, joining several other missionary families. The ensuing six years of mission work were exciting. Located in The Hague, the church grew from two to seventy. The church built a new church building during our fifth year.

After six exciting, involved years, Ray and I felt it was time to return to the United States. After serving as minister for two different churches, Ray was offered a teaching position in a school of ministry in Dallas—his second dream come true.

During our short time with the school, we became quite close to the students and their families. We were very happy—it was nearly a perfect existence for us.

Then, in February of 1979, Ray, along with three other teachers in the school—Eldred Stephens, Rudell White, and Tom Dockery—left early one morning in a private plane to attend a Bible lectureship. Two days later at 4:30 A.M. on February 21, 1979, my doorbell rang. When the doorbell woke me from my sleep, my first thought was that Ray was home. I conjectured that he must have left his house keys at home and was now locked out. But when I opened the door, I saw a policeman standing there. He asked if I was Mrs. Ray Evans. After I stated that I was, he asked if he might come in because "it's foggy tonight." I knew instantly something bad had happened.

"Just tell me. How bad is it?" I pleaded.

"The plane crashed, and all the men have been killed." My shock was great; my pain was like a knife cutting through my heart. For the second time, I was suddenly and unexpectedly a widow.

I felt an immediate need to go to the three other new widows. I got in my car and drove to two of their homes (the third lived farther away).

For the second time, I was suddenly and unexpectedly a widow.

When I returned home, I woke up our high school senior, Kirby—who was our youngest child and the only one still at home—to tell him the news. At 6:30 A.M., I began to call my family and to hear from friends. I felt strangely empowered by my first loss. I knew that I, once again, would survive and regain control of my life. My faith was unshaken; God would see me through.

After the funeral, Kirby returned to school and I to my work as a receptionist. At the time, I didn't realize how dysfunctional I was. I'd find myself in a room not knowing how I got there. Someone would give me information and I would soon forget it. I would sleep for only two hours during the night and feel exhausted the next day. I would dream that Ray was explaining to me that the plane crash had not happened. Upon awakening, I'd be devastated. How was I going to get through this? I prayed; Oh, how I prayed. "Please Lord, see me through this." Reading Scripture did not help, even though I knew I was supposed to find comfort there. How often I had read Hebrews 13:5: "I will never leave you, nor forsake you." But where was the comfort I was supposed to have?

I pondered again and again the question put to me by a dear friend: "JoAnn, what will your ministry be? You are no longer the wife of a preacher or teacher; your role will be different." After Kirby graduated from high school, I returned to Oklahoma and found that our congregation had no program to meet the needs of single men and women. Twelve single ladies began regularly meeting. During the next four years, most of my strength came from weekly meetings with these single women. I was able to strengthen them and they me.

No one can endure the intense pain for you.

Again, ultimately, healing occurred. I developed a new relationship with a wonderful man, and we married. We now have a most blessed existence. Our families have blended well, and my husband and I are both actively working for the Lord.

Although I have twice experienced sudden and unexpected loss, both times my life has returned to joy, optimism, and involvement. For those facing a similar journey, you must know that your pathway will be clouded, uncertain, and difficult. The loss of a mate, child, or parent presents seemingly insurmountable obstacles, and the journey toward healing will be the most difficult trek you will ever undertake. No one can go in your place, no one can endure the intense pain for you, no one can bear the loneliness of the night for you, no one can take away the emptiness of the loss, no one can fill the empty shoes or comfort your troubled heart.

God will carry you when you can't walk.

However, God will carry you when you can't walk. You will find his loving arms wrapped around you when your heart is hard and devoid of love.

It was three years before I was finally able to say, "Ray is dead; he will not be coming back." I began putting my life back together. After this period of shock and intense grieving was over, I began to see how God had been working in my life. Through it all, God provided support, avenues of opportunity, and emotional strength—fortified by a foundation of faith. My disappointment, loss, sense of tragedy, and dissolution of relationships ultimately resulted in spiritual and personal growth. When I couldn't pray, God gave me friends. When I couldn't sing, he gave me my church family. When I needed love, he gave me his love and peace. Finally, he gave me someone to love again.

—JoAnn Belknap

In Memory of *Rob and Gene*

My husband, Gene, was a welder by trade and owned a large fabricating and heat treatment plant, but he had many other interests and hobbies. One of his hobbies was stock car racing, a pastime he began enjoying as a teenager. Our oldest son, Rob, was also keenly interested in racing. Rob built his own cars and knew a great deal about how they should handle.

Because of his expertise, Rob lost his life in 1983 while test-driving another man's car. This tragedy devastated our family.

Certain people kept telling me, "Now, Flo, you know that 'all things happen for good to them that love the Lord.'" I was so angry, so bitter, and so hurt by their telling me this that I determined to find out where that verse was in the Bible and then ask the Lord what he meant by putting such a statement in my Bible! I wasn't angry about Rob's death—crushed by it, yes, but not angry. I was so thankful that the Lord had given him to us in the first place that I couldn't be angry. But I was angry about that passage and at those people for telling it to me. Well, I found it in the eighth chapter of Romans. But it doesn't read at all like they were quoting it. It's really a most wonderful passage and has been my mainstay for the last twelve years.

When I read the eighth chapter of Romans now, I feel very close to God. I am his and he is mine. I've been adopted; I am part of his family; he knows me; I am his child. I no longer need to be fearful because my Father is there. And when I suffer and hurt, as all creation does from time to time, he will be there. Even when I am so confused, so devastated by my circumstances that I don't know what to do, the Holy Spirit is there for me. He will interpret my deepest thoughts, needs, and prayers and present them to the Lord for me. He is there to help me overcome, grow, and know that, even though this bad thing has happened, he will help me. And, if I rely on him, I will emerge victorious, strengthened by his power, with a deeper faith and more godliness than before.

After reading Romans 8 over and over again, I had a dream. This dream has encouraged me and given me strength and hope that I never thought I could have. A "person" or angel was walking toward me with arms outstretched, crying. He held me, and we cried together. Perhaps it was Robbie, but whoever it was, I know that when I woke up I was still crying, and I knew instantly that God understood my grief and was crying too. He isn't a vindictive God; he is my loving Father—and fathers hurt when their children hurt.

Gene and I adopted Romans 8 as the theme of our lives. *Nothing* can separate us from the love of Christ—not trouble, not hardship, not grief. "No, in all these things we are more than conquerors through [Christ] who loved us" (Rom. 8:37).

My faith in this verse was put to the test on September 26, 1993. That Sunday morning after church, Gene went home alone, while I stayed at church to attend a ladies' meeting.

When I woke up I was still crying, and I knew instantly that God understood my grief and was crying too.

When I called him, he didn't answer the phone; so I guessed that he might be cutting the grass. I left a message on the recorder: "Honey, would you please check your calendar. Marlin and Carolyn would like to go out to dinner next Friday night. I'll be home in a few minutes." Carolyn and I finished checking our calendars and left. As we drove into the driveway, I thought it strange that the grass hadn't been cut and that the garage door was closed; the house seemed so silent. As Carolyn drove away, I let myself in the front door and called his name. No response. I went toward the kitchen, and there I saw him lying on the floor. For an instant I thought he was playing a joke on me, but, no, this was real. Again, I called his name and asked, "What happened?" He raised up and said something about his arm. He was cold and wet—like someone had poured water on him.

From then on everything played out in my mind as though I were watching a movie: 911, the neighbor who's a fireman, the medics, the ambulance, the emergency room. I couldn't catch my breath. Our son Steve was concerned because there was no pulse in Gene's arm. That strong arm that we'd always depended on . . . his welding arm . . . his shooting arm . . . his loving arm. "Please doctor, fix his arm." But there were far more serious concerns than his arm.

I'll never forget the look on our daughter Brenda's face as she tried to get through the automatic glass doors into the emergency room. She looked like a little, trapped, frightened animal—Daddy's girl, Daddy's little angel.

Gene died about 2:30 A.M. after going on the heart/lung machine while they tried to repair the damage. The aorta wouldn't hold; nothing more could be done. The doctors were so kind, so experienced, and so skilled, but when an aorta ruptures the damage is extensive.

It had happened again. Our dear loved one had been taken from us. Without warning, without a last good-bye—stolen as if by a thief in the night.

I move through life in a haze, sometimes coping, other times simply following my children's suggestions.

I move through life in a haze, sometimes coping, other times simply following my children's suggestions. They are fine Christian adults who rely on the Lord's strength.

Some have questioned why I'm not angry at God. I have never been angry— though sometimes I wonder, myself, why I'm not angry. When Gene died, I fell back on the assurances of

Romans 8—our life theme. I'm just sure that Jesus is mine and that I am his. This belief is the anchor in my life.

At a concert held in Gene's honor, the Christian singing group Acappella sang a song that describes my faith. This song, "More than Conquerors" (used by permission), was written by Bill and Janny Grien.

> We've been made more than conquerors,
> Overcomers in this life.
> We've been made victorious through the blood of
>   Jesus Christ.
>
> When trouble comes knocking at your door, don't be
>   afraid.
> You know it's not like before.
> Don't you give in, don't let it bring you down.
> You don't have to worry any more.
>
> We've been made more than conquerors,
> Overcomers in this life.
> We've been made victorious through the blood of
>   Jesus Christ.
>
> Hold on, we're getting stronger every day.
> There's no reason for you to go astray.
> Don't go leaning to your understanding
> 'Cause you don't have to worry anyway.
>
> We've been made more than conquerors;
> Overcomers in this life.
> We've been made victorious through the blood of
>   Jesus Christ.

In my mind's eye I see Gene walking through a field of grain at his farm in Bowling Green. The sun is shining brightly and is glistening off the sweat on his broad shoulders. He has on his tan shorts and a blue tank top with that old Willie Nelson bandanna around his head. He has his eye on something in the distance, as he's pushing through the heads of grain. He's striving onward and upward toward his Father. He doesn't realize the heartache he left behind. He doesn't hear our cries because he hears a higher calling, the one he has heard all of his life. Now, he's almost there.

Loved ones come to fill the gap, but only time can dull the ache. I hear a song from time to time that says "All those lonely nights without you, just one more time, let me put my arms around you." Someday, I may be able to do that, but I don't think it will be important anymore. We will have reached the goal.

—Flo Rowland

Voices from the Storm of Terror

❧

INTRODUCTION

> What I feared has come upon me;
> what I dreaded has happened to me.
> (Job 3:25)

Terror! Not all of us have experienced it, but all of us fear it.

We all have something that we dread most in life. How would you respond if what you dreaded actually happened to you?

At first, the shock of the terror numbs the senses and confuses reality. But then, as the numbness wears off and reality comes into focus, the pain—the enormous pain—begins to take hold. Where is the justice? Where is the goodness? Where is God? How can faith survive?

The three stories in this chapter bring to life some of the nightmares that we all dread. Terry Rush shares his experience in the vicious murder of his daughter's fiancé. Shock, sadness, pain, uncertainty—these are just some of the emotions Terry shares with us. The second story is of the brutal rape of a young Christian woman, Julie Lindsey. Julie shares her fear, her experience, and her faith. Julie's insights into why bad things happen to good people provide hope for us all. Finally, we hear from, Don Rogers, a survivor of the infamous Oklahoma City bombing of the Alfred P. Murrah Federal Building. His terrifying story reminds us that none of us know what tomorrow holds.

From all three of these brave storm survivors, we hear that God is good, that he is a God who can be trusted. Through their experiences of terror, they learned what countless others have learned throughout history—that our God will never forsake us.

> Be strong and courageous. Do not be afraid or terrified because of them, for the Lord your God goes with you; he will never leave you nor forsake you. (Deut. 31:6)

Terry's TERROR

The evening of December 7, 1992, best I recall, had a cool crisp edge in the air. Mary and I returned home from a Christmas play to find a note from our daughter, Wendy, that was not in the least bit alarming. "Have gone with Mark McCoy. Will call you later." Simple enough.

Little did we know that behind those two simple sentences was the unleashing of hellish terror and pain. Just moments later the phone rang. Its message, now months later, is still all too clear.

In a very deliberate voice, our dear neighbor, Judy McCoy, carefully spaced each word. "Terry-I'm-so-sorry-to-tell-you-this—Something-terrible-has-happened—Wendy's boyfriend-has-been-killed—And-Terry-it-wasn't-an-accident—It-looks-like-someone-has-murdered-him-and-his-brother—Mark-has-taken-Wendy-to-the-scene—I-am-so-sorry-to-have-to-tell-you-this-Terry—I-am-so-sorry—."

I thanked her the best I could, and in shock, hung up.

Although I remained standing, I couldn't verify that there was a floor beneath me. I picked up where Judy's cadence left off and repeated the message to Mary. This information was too stunning to be heard, let alone be true.

Although I remained standing, I couldn't verify that there was a floor beneath me.

I just stood. My first thought was, "God, how should I handle this?" It was too hard to hear. I had to call Judy back and ask her to repeat everything she had just said to be certain I had heard her right.

Twenty-six year old Bobby Phillips was engaged to Wendy. He had called from work that evening and was to be at our house by seven. But first, he had to run home and change clothes.

Although I had heard Judy twice, I still thought she must have had the story wrong. Most likely the boys had been badly hurt . . . but not killed. I was pretty sure someone had gotten a little over anxious and had exaggerated parts of the story.

Mary and I headed immediately for Bobby's house. The night air had turned soupy with fog. The speedometer read 55 mph. But it seemed the car was moving so much slower. My hips and legs didn't have any feeling. Neither of us said much in the car. One would mumble something about Wendy. Much later another would ask what the possibility was that someone had simply misunderstood. Maybe it wasn't a murder, but rather an accident. Maybe he wasn't dead. Not Bobby.

I didn't think we would ever get to his house. On the other hand, I didn't want to get there.

We wove through the heavy fog that lulled the streets into quiet slumber. The closer we got, the more anxious we became. Shock seemed to make everything too strange. My whole being felt as out of place as an arm that goes to sleep in the middle of the night. This was all too wrong.

It was a strain to read the street signs. As we found the entrance to their housing addition, an ambulance was leaving. We moaned. Shortly, we came around a corner, and the fog was pierced by a staggering scene.

Squad cars with their kaleidoscopic flashing lights were everywhere. Yellow tape rudely barricaded the Phillips' lawn and house against the rest of the neighborhood. Enormous, gigantic sickness rushed in and drowned my heart. It was true.

My whole being felt as out of place as an arm that goes to sleep in the middle of the night. This was all too wrong.

Light beamed from every room of the house. The roof-line and shrubbery were dancing with strings of Christmas lights. The house itself spoke of irony. Something was brightly wrong.

Reporters moved about doing their job. Television crews, along with trucks and equipment, added to the overwhelming assurance that Judy's words were, after all, true.

We approached a neighboring house that was being used as "police headquarters." I really preferred not to step through the door. We entered into massive heartbreak. Bobby's parents, Wanda and Bob, sat on a sofa. Wanda sat with her arm around Bob, who was slumped in tears. His jacket was stained with Bobby's blood. A police chaplain somewhat anchored the room while the policemen and policewomen continually moved back and forth between this house and the Phillips'.

I found Wendy in the next room with Mark McCoy. She was white. Her countenance was totally blank. Her heart was blown away. Her fiancé was dead. Words were futile; their combinations did little to mend the moment. Hugs, tears, broken sentences, and a lot of coffee filled the hours ahead.

Words were futile; their combinations did little to mend the moment.

Intermittent sobbing verified that the night was filled with grievous disorientation. In and out . . . in and out—the detectives were hustling. The woman whose home we were using ministered sweetly to us: "The phone is clear now. Would anyone care for more coffee?"

Mary stayed with Wendy. I moved from Wendy, to Bob and Wanda, to the phone, and then circled again . . . and again. I called my boys and told them what I couldn't bear for them to hear. Mostly, I sat with Wendy on the floor against an out-of-the-way bare wall. Maryann and Brad (Bobby's sister and her husband) came in from an otherwise enjoyable evening to be pelted with the worst. It was unbearable to watch this evening unfurl its nightmarish saga.

Police worked in overdrive, while the rest of us sat with glazed eyes and did our best to think of something intelligent to say. I heard one officer ask Bob and Wanda if they owned an ax. What in the world had happened to our boy?

The events of the double murder remain sketchy. Bobby's nineteen-year-old brother, David, had been home alone. David was mentally handicapped. At approximately 5:00 P.M. someone had entered the house, had shot David in the head, and had then strangled him. It is possible that when Bobby came home, he noticed that something was dangerously wrong.

It appears that he entered from the garage into the kitchen, picking up an ax along the way. The intruder(s) turned the weapon on him and also stabbed him. This clean-cut, handsome, hardworking boy was ruthlessly bludgeoned to his death.

The next few days were treacherous. At night, wails muffled by her pillow could be heard coming from Wendy's room. Sometimes there would be a shift into perpetual sobbing. Her terrifying nightmares would awaken us all.

Our world of friends overwhelmed us with warmth, compassion, and love. The Phillipses, too, were bombarded with consoling strength from those who loved them. The grief was suffocating all the while. It killed me to know why people constantly brought food to the house. Flowers were everywhere . . . absolutely everywhere.

Television reporters repeatedly came to our home for interviews. Other media would call wanting to know the floor plans to the Phillips' house, etc. I believe the worst experience of my life was when I took Wendy to the funeral home. Due to the blows to Bobby's head, whether the family should view his body was undecided. A couple of his cousins and I went in first to determine if others should follow. Viewing was permitted.

The right side of the skull had received extensive trauma. Wendy continually patted his face and felt his arms and chest. Suddenly she said, "Daddy, look at this over here." She was pointing to the undamaged left side of his head and face. "Look how smooth it is over here. Could we turn him around?"

It took a lot of explaining to convince her that we could not. With a certain peace, she sighed, "Oh well, I'm just going to always remember the good side."

December 11 presented a picture too baffling. The pace of pain seemed to gain speed and weight. Tom Bedicek, the minister of Bob and Wanda's church, opened the services of the double funeral. Mitch Wilburn, David's youth minister, spoke in honor of David. I was privileged to preach the funeral of Bobby, who had become my own son.

It was only and literally by the genuine assistance of God that we functioned.

To look into the eyes of family and friends was incomprehensible. We three men didn't have the strength to carry this load. There was an unspoken respect for each other's brokenness. It was only and literally by the genuine assistance of God that we functioned. Each was conscious, and that was the extent of our strength for the moment.

Once again, there was no feeling in my hips or legs. Unsure whether I was making contact with the floor, I felt a floating sensation. I kept feeling as if I might collapse and feared that Tom and Mitch would be forced to hold me up while I addressed those packed into the church building.

The days following were streams of bewilderment. Numbness sometimes showed signs of dissipating. I felt extremely close to God. He was doing the work, for I was far too weak to function. The Lord was always strong; I never was. Sorrow flooded my mind, heart, and soul.

Chaos ensued. Detectives warned the Phillipses and us that additional lives might be at risk. Guard dogs were brought into both homes. For days, the local news interviewed Bobby and David's family, Wendy, and myself. For weeks after the incident, it was not unusual to hear the radio announcer say: "The latest on the murder of Bobby and David Phillips . . ." Sometimes I could take it.

When I came home in the evenings, I would often find Mary sitting in the dark, replaying the events in her mind. Sometimes I would find Wendy folded in tears on her bed. But even so, only moments later, Wendy would say something that would let me know she was going to come through this. We were always aware that Bob, Wanda, Maryann, and Brad were across town, also feeling stunned and hurt. Everyday I expected to be done crying. I did well in front of people . . . sometimes. I cried the hardest and hottest and the longest in the shower. I felt like something must be wrong with me, that I shouldn't be this devastated. I finally had to quit telling myself that I wouldn't cry anymore. I still cry.

I don't know what others thought of how we were doing. I don't know how we ought to have done. God was doing good in us, though.

How painful is pain! How unacceptable is this which we are forced to accept! Was there a plug we could pull to make all of this stop? Did anyone know of a rewind button? How could this happen? This stuff happens to others, not us. None of us received any warning. There were no yellow lights of caution to prepare us for this unfathomable intersection.

I finally had to quit telling myself that I wouldn't cry anymore. I still cry.

"So, Terry, where was this God you say loves us? Where was his compassion? And of what benefit was your faith?" These haunting questions are the reason I reveal my story to you.

The events I share with you reveal multiple personal weaknesses found in me. I share my story that you may know the glory and beauty and power of God. The radiance of the diamond shows up best when placed against the darkest cloth.

Grief can't choke out our hope if God has our permission to spend that hope. Rather, grief gives way to delight and eventual joy. What I have experienced has been wonderfully privileged and blessed. I have tasted ruin. God has hurried to help. He has made a way when there seemed to be no way.

I can't say that we ever get over significant loss. By his work in us, though, we do get on. We move forward with great tears, assured healing, enormous sorrow, comfort from the Spirit, painful reminders, happy reminders, and hope.

As you try to pick up the pieces of your own personal terror, I give my support. When you stare off into endless space, I gaze there myself. When you talk of the deceased as if they were alive (having momentarily forgotten they are not), I have done the same. When your tears have nearly drowned you and your mind won't quit rehashing the series of events, I have communion with your pain.

I have tasted ruin. God has hurried to help.

Therefore, I insist . . . when there seems to be no way, God will make a way. Hope is on its way . . . from above!

—Terry Rush (from his book, *God Will Make a Way*)

Julie's TERROR

Working the late shift that spring night in 1985 at the Days Inn just south of Montgomery, Alabama, I never imagined that my life was about to change through a most horrible experience. I'd recently moved to Montgomery to finish college and start a professional career. The hotel job helped pay the bills as I finished school.

Just after 11 P.M., two men came to the registration desk where I worked alone. They asked about a room for the night. As I turned to look at the motel diagram for a vacancy, one of them produced a pistol and pointed it at my head.

I wanted to scream but I couldn't. I couldn't move. I was paralyzed with fear. I could hardly breathe I was so frightened. The one holding the gun told me to act natural and do as he told me.

They both walked behind the counter and cleaned out the cash register. I felt the gun pressed into my spine. He was standing so close behind me I could feel his breath on my neck. He grabbed my arm and told me we were going for a ride.

I begged him not to hurt me. He told me I wouldn't get hurt as long as I did what I was told, but that if I didn't, he'd use his gun on me.

The three of us walked to their car. One man got into the back, while the gunman forced me into the passenger side of the front seat. He never took his eyes off me as he walked around to the driver's side and got in.

He pulled onto the interstate and proceeded south at a high rate of speed. I remember that the radio was on, and they were singing. They kept asking me if I knew where more money was. I finally convinced them I didn't. I assured them they had gotten all the money there was.

The man in the back seat leaned up and put his hand down my shirt. He then pulled me into the back seat and forced me to perform oral sex. He kept asking me if I thought I was too good, and he kept calling me names. I prayed I wouldn't be sick.

The driver kept threatening to use the gun on me if I didn't do what they told me. Finally, he let me up and pushed me back into the front seat.

The driver then demanded oral sex. It was all I could do not to throw up.

He pushed me over to the passenger side of the car. He pulled off the road and told me to get out of the car. He threatened to shoot me if I didn't. I got out and he followed. He grabbed my arm and led me into the woods while the other man stayed in the car.

He stopped me in front of a tree and handcuffed me. He walked around behind me and raped me. I kept praying for it to be over. He was brutal and he delighted in hurting me. I began to think about what it was going to be like when he killed me. I really believed he was going to shoot me.

I prayed to live. I thought about my family and friends and how they would feel knowing I had died such a horrible death. I thought of all the things I hadn't said or done. I didn't want to die this way.

I began to think about what it was going to be like when he killed me.

When he finally finished raping me, I closed my eyes and waited for him to kill me. He took my jewelry and began walking away from me. He turned and told me he would call someone and tell them where I was. Then he left.

My whole body sagged in relief. I couldn't believe he'd left me alive. I heard him get in the car and drive away. I fell to the ground and just lay there. I couldn't think. I didn't know what to do. I kept telling myself to think.

Finally, it came to me that he probably wasn't going to call anyone to tell them where I was. I also thought he might think twice about letting me live and come back after me.

I found my way to the highway. At two in the morning there's not much traffic. I tried to flag down a couple of cars. They wouldn't stop. Thinking back on it, I can't really blame them.

Eventually a truck driver stopped and called for a state trooper over the radio.

Arriving policemen took me to the hospital and then to the police station. In shock, I endured the examinations, the confiscation of my tattered clothes for evidence, and the repetitive barrage of questions. It was after daylight before the police allowed my sister to take me back to Montgomery.

Though my nightmare began suddenly, it drug on for months. The hotel fired me. I dropped out of school. I just couldn't function. Everything I did was a major effort and every decision monumental. I was shattered, lost, and bewildered.

I just couldn't function. Everything I did was a major effort and every decision monumental. I was shattered, lost, and bewildered.

A few weeks after the assault, I sat outside the meeting room of the Grand Jury of Montgomery County, Alabama. The police had caught my rapists a few days earlier and I had picked them out of a lineup, signing warrants for their arrests. The Grand Jury was meeting to decide whether to indict them. Before testifying, I paced the worn floor tiles nervously. I was afraid and distraught. The two robber/rapists had committed a series of crimes while traveling down an interstate through the southeastern United States. I kept wondering, "Why did they come back here? They'd gone hundreds of miles and had committed many more crimes before they came back. Of all the people they've assaulted, why do I have to be the one to face them in a courtroom? I'm scared. Why do I have to live this awful thing all over again?"

The two detectives working my case assured me I wouldn't see the rapists that day; they said I would go before the jury alone. The detectives also predicted that I wouldn't have to face the rapists in a courtroom and endure the pain of telling my story as they sat watching me with hatred and threats in their eyes. The detectives thought the pair would seek the best possible deal with the court through a plea bargain. I'm glad they predicted correctly. Both criminals now serve sentences in Holman prison in Atmore, Alabama. One is eligible for parole in the year 2000. The other in 2001.

After this experience, I spent a great deal of time thinking about God, my relationship with him, and what I believe about him. I searched and I prayed for understanding. I longed to be healed, and I wanted desperately to feel the power of God's presence. My spirit and my faith were sorely tested; my spiritual journey in the months that followed was painful—and also wonderful.

It seemed to me this event was a classic case of good versus evil—an event that led to the infamous question of why bad things happen to good people. But it finally occurred to me that the question was not "why me?" as much as "why not me?" God didn't promise me that nothing bad would ever happen to me. His own Son was crucified, suffering the cruelest death known to man.

Do I believe God could have stopped this tragedy from happening to me? Absolutely. The question is: Why didn't he? I believe God wants me to love, honor and serve him because I choose to. God has never forced himself on me or made me serve him. He certainly has the power to do so. But the Almighty God, who could annihilate the universe with a mere thought, gave his creation free will. I have the gift of choosing. But as I have choices, so do others. Choices have consequences. Choices have blessings. If I accept the concept that I have free will, I must also accept that the two men who raped me have free will as well.

But it finally occurred to me that the question was not "why me?" as much as "why not me?"

God wants a real and honest relationship with me. In order for that kind of relationship to exist, I must choose it. God gave us the choices from the very beginning. I had often wondered why God placed the tree of knowledge of good and evil right in the middle of the Garden and then told Adam and Eve not to eat from it. Now I understand that God was giving them a choice about whether to obey him and believe him.

The two men who raped me made a different choice than I, and our choices came into conflict. It would appear that I had been overcome and that Satan had triumphed by inflicting great pain and damage into my life. And for awhile, that's how I felt.

But then the blessings of choosing God came! God allowed me to profit from an awful and devastating event. So many good things are in my life now. I have wonderful friends—most of whom I would never have met or known were it not for this experience. I have a job that allows me to work with and serve crime victims. I have a deeper relationship with God. I am spiritually wiser and more mature. I have been blessed beyond what I can tell in these pages, and I am very grateful. Romans 8:28 came alive in my life: "All things work together for good to them that love God, [and] are called according to his purpose."

I chose God and he did not fail me. I continue to recover, and God continues to teach me. The two men who raped me did not choose God and were a vessel of Satan to do harm. They are both serving lengthy prison terms in a maximum security facility. They and their families suffer as a result.

Now I ask you—who won?

STORY THREE

Don's TERROR

The bombing of the Alfred P. Murrah Federal Building was one of the most horrific man-made disasters in the history of the United States. I was in the first-floor lobby, just outside my office, of that building at 9:02 A.M., April 19, 1995. Beyond the immediate crisis of survival, as manager for the federal complex, I was concerned for the well-being of my employees, the day-care children, and the building tenants. I was also responsible for any possible preservation of the building. In the following hours, days, and weeks, the crisis demanded that I deal with the deaths and life-threatening injuries of many employees, as well as the emotional trauma suffered by the surviving employees and the victims' families. I had been there when ground was broken for construction of the Murrah Federal Building and had played a major role in the management of the building for nineteen years. I cared for that building from its cradle to its grave. Witnessing the loss of lives, critical injuries, and destruction of the building was devastating to me.

My office was on the north side of the first floor. I had just concluded a meeting in my office and had walked out to the lobby with one of the meeting participants when the blast hit me. The smoke surrounded me and covered me with complete darkness. I choked and gasped for air. I heard a voice call my name. I couldn't see, but I reached for the sound of the voice. I found the arm of the person I had been standing with before the blast, and he crawled through the rubble and falling debris toward me. We felt our way inch by inch, as if we were in a deep cavern, not knowing what lay before us. I started to think that I wasn't going to get out, but I just kept going, holding my breath, hoping to find a way out. We climbed through the rubble for about eighty feet and came across two women, who were confusedly moving toward the interior of the building. We helped them out and exited the west side of the building through the large overhead dock door that had been blown off.

The smoke surrounded me and covered me with complete darkness. I choked and gasped for air.

After turning around to look at the front of the building, I wondered how we had been able to escape. Smoke poured out. The front entrance was blown inward. A large gaping hole was all that remained where approximately one-half of the building had stood. On the street about twenty-five cars were on fire. I couldn't imagine what could have caused such terrible damage. I immediately ran to the south entrance to try to enter the building. Men were using makeshift ladders from playground fences to climb into the building to try to rescue those still inside. The east stairwell was so blocked by rubble that I couldn't walk up the stairs. I climbed back down and looked up.

I saw a man pinned against a wall, hanging out of the building. Half of the top of his head was gone. The lower portion of his body was completely crushed; as he looked up, all he could say was, "Help me. Please help me." A moment later, his life was gone. The federal workers who were trying to pull him out looked at each other in a frightened, horrible, helpless way, knowing nothing could be done. Although my eyes were full of smoke, dust and debris, I remember clearly viewing this man's death struggle.

I remember clearly viewing this man's death struggle.

By this time, the fire department had arrived and started their rescue efforts. I tried to get into the building again to search for some of the other victims because I knew where they were. My shirt was torn, and I had cuts all over my body. The firefighters saw me in the building, and two of them took me out. I told them that I had to try to find some of the other victims, but they wouldn't let me go back inside. Within a few minutes, I was taken to the emergency room of Saint Anthony Hospital, located near the bombing site. As I lay on the gurney, waiting for them to treat my injuries, I realized that I was in shock. I felt tremendous guilt because I was still alive when there were so many who weren't. I also felt guilty that I hadn't been able to rescue more than the ones that I had helped out. As I lay there, watching the nurses and doctors going from gurney to gurney helping people, I felt a sudden peace, as if the Holy Spirit were telling me that I had no reason to feel guilty. My heavenly Father gave me peace in the knowledge that I had done all that I could do.

I felt tremendous guilt because I was still alive when there were so many who weren't.

After being released from the hospital several hours later, I reunited with my wife, who, along with my three brothers, had been searching for me. We gathered together and said a prayer of thanks, acknowledging that my life was spared for a purpose known only by God. Then I went back to the building site to set up a command center for emergency operations. Later that night, I went into the building with the Phoenix Fire Department Rescue Team to try to locate and identify bodies in the rubble in the interior part of the building. A light mist was falling, and it was cold when we prepared to enter the building from the south entrance. The rescue team took each of our names and tagged us. This way, if the building collapsed, they would know which rescue team members were still inside the building. I remember thinking that this couldn't be the same building that I had worked in for nineteen years. It was hard to identify anything; it seemed as if we were going down into a large cavern with debris heaped up on the ground and hanging from the ceiling.

One of my employees was with me when we finally climbed over to the bodies. He looked at two of the bodies, which he could not identify. I looked at a third body a few yards away. I asked the Phoenix Fire Department Chaplain, "How do you expect me to identify this body? It doesn't even look like a person." He told me that it was a woman wearing a black dress with roses imprinted on it. He could tell by the shreds of material he saw embedded in the rocks and crevices. I looked around with a flashlight and found the place where I had been standing when the blast went off. It was only a few feet away from that woman. I couldn't take my eyes off her—that human being lying in a grave of stone, that twisted mass that was once a beautiful person. As I looked at her remains, I remembered seeing a woman in a black dress imprinted with roses get off the elevator on the first floor and walk past me just before the blast went off.

At the time of this writing, several months have passed. I still have dreadful dreams and haunting remembrances every day. I still replay those horrible sights over and over in my mind. Sometimes I wonder why I am alive when 168 others are in their graves. I sometimes wonder about how well any one of us in that building was prepared for that fateful day. I know the children from the day-care were innocent, and they are in God's hands. I knew many of the people who perished well enough to know that they were prepared to die, but I don't know about the others. This causes me the most grief when I think about the deaths resulting from that bomb.

Chapter 12 of Acts tells how Herod the King arrested Peter and threw him into prison, delivering him to four squads of soldiers, who were charged with guarding him.

> The night before Herod was to bring him to trial, Peter was sleeping between two soldiers, bound with two chains, and sentries stood guard at the entrance. Suddenly an angel of the Lord appeared and a light shone in the cell. He struck Peter on the side and woke him up. "Quick, get up!" he said, and the chains fell off Peter's wrists.
>
> Then the angel said to him, "Put on your clothes and sandals." And Peter did so. "Wrap your cloak around you and follow me." (Acts 12:6–8)

Do we go to sleep at night prepared for the fate of the next day?

It amazes me that Peter was able to fall asleep that night. Most likely, he understood that the next day he would meet the same fate as James did in the hands of Herod. Would we be able to sleep knowing that the next day our lives would be taken? Peter had established his faith in Jesus Christ, which granted him security about his destiny. Do we go to sleep at night prepared for the fate of the next day?

—Don Rogers

CHAPTER 3

Voices from the Storm of **Divorce**

❧

INTRODUCTION

Many who have experienced the storm of divorce feel that death would have been easier. Divorce doesn't carry the finality that death does, but death doesn't create the feelings of rejection and failure that divorce frequently arouses. Most who suffer through an unwanted divorce, forever ask the question, "What if . . . ?"

Divorce comes to men and women of all ages, in all social and economic brackets. It hurts all who endure it. Among Christians, divorce is often condemned—and those struggling beneath an already crippling load are strapped with yet another burden.

Introduction

They are frequently ostracized and excluded; they are viewed with suspicion and even fear. The stories in this chapter are written by men and women who love God and desire to live according to his plan, but Satan worked havoc in their lives and tore apart marriages that God wanted to last a lifetime.

The last names of the storytellers in this chapter will not be revealed. Those who tell their stories have no desire to hurt their ex-spouses or damage their reputations. Many of the first names have been changed as well.

The brave souls who write these stories have opened their hearts and revealed their pain. Because they were willing to be vulnerable, others going through the storm of divorce will find comfort and hope.

Scott's STORY

It was particularly cold that Saturday, even for February, yet I was oblivious to the wind. My heart was racing and my mind was spinning as I stumbled across the field behind our house. My wife of one-and-a-half years had told me something that morning that had shattered everything that was important to me, and a growing sense of claustrophobia had driven me outside to try to piece things back together.

In many respects we were a typical, young Christian couple. Our common faith had drawn us together. The time we spent together in worship and small group Bible studies assured us that our commitment to each other would be as strong as our commitment to God. We had gone through premarital counseling and felt a growing confidence that we were making right choices. I taught at a Christian high school, helped lead a campus ministry, and participated in a Christian drama ministry. My wife was actively involved in these activities with me. I had learned what it meant to have a "suitable helper." She shared my interests and allowed me to share hers.

The birth of our son eleven months after our wedding seemed to complete the portrait. We were no longer a couple, but a family, and we were excited about nurturing our children and helping them mature toward the same spiritual goals we had.

But on this morning, as I struggled for breath in the barren fields behind our home, all these memories, these hopes, seemed forever out of reach. There had been growing tension in our relationship over the past few months, and I was at a loss about how to change it. Communication had shut down, feelings were worn on sleeves, and anger seemed to explode out of nowhere. It was clear to me that these changes must have come from somewhere, but my wife kept assuring me that I was wrong. Finally, I felt I could no longer take the stress of our struggling relationship. There had to be a cause, and I was determined to discover it.

On that Saturday morning we sat together on the sofa and talked. As she struggled for words, I saw in her eyes what I had dreaded, and I prepared myself for the worst. There was another man—they were in love—it had been going on for a long time—she was sorry. As I think back, I am surprised at the variety of feelings I had. Of course, I was shocked and hurt, but I also felt a certain peace. At least I knew I wasn't crazy for imagining all the turmoil. However, the worst wasn't over yet. There was one more thing. Our son . . . my son . . . wasn't mine.

How do you deal with something like this? At that point, you don't. It was all I could do just to take it all in. Even then, it seemed like a soap opera story, and I waited desperately for the commercial break. As I walked alone in the field, each breath of cold air seemed to slap my mind into consciousness. This was no dream. What do I do? Is my marriage over? Do I have a son? How do I tell my parents? How will this affect my job? One thing was sure—I was no longer one of the "safely marrieds." The legacy shared by my parents and their parents ended with me. I had a troubled marriage, and it would forever change my life.

There was another man—they were in love—it had been going on for a long time—she was sorry.

My wife was surprised by my response to her confession. She was sure that truth would give her the freedom she wanted, but I was determined not to let go so easily. I was going to fight for my marriage and my family. Of course, I reacted out of several motives. I knew that this affair was wrong and that this man could not lead her closer to Christ. I knew my son needed a Christian home and that our marriage was his only hope for one. Most of all, I reacted out of desperation. I didn't want to lose this chance for happiness. I didn't want to be lonely.

For the next two months, I tried everything within my power to win back the marriage I had lost. Though we were separated, I sent cards and flowers; I called and visited her. I took every opportunity to make my case. I tested the promises of prayer and talked with God like never before. Since the Bible says that the prayers of righteous people are powerful and effective, I determined to get as many righteous people as possible to pray for me. I tried to take advantage of every opportunity, to use every tool in my spiritual arsenal, to enlist every friend and counselor. But day after day, the handwriting on the wall became clearer. Satan had won not only my wife's heart, but the battle as well. In May of that year, we both stood before a judge and received his final decree. The divorce was granted.

The year, 1986—the year the divorce was finalized—was an exhausting one. I felt as if I went through the entire year in high gear, every nerve at attention, every muscle tied in knots. Sleep was a welcome relief, but it was often disrupted. I vividly remember waking up each morning, feeling relaxed and invigorated. Then suddenly, I would remember what had occurred and what I had to face that day. The tension would begin before I got out of bed and would continue all day until I finally went to sleep again. I just couldn't escape it.

> I went through the entire year in high gear, every nerve at attention, every muscle tied in knots.

As far as work was concerned, all I can say is that I was there. Each day, I got out of bed, already exhausted, and went to work. I did very little teaching, gave many assignments, and allowed the students to enjoy a lot of free time. I knew that I was a much better teacher than that, but I just didn't have the energy or the attention span to do lesson plans, grade projects, or spend the quality time necessary to really teach. Other teachers helped pick up some slack, and even the students understood and helped out as much as they could.

It was a very lonely year for me as well. In fact, had it not been for great Christian friends who allowed me to sleep on their sofas and share their friendship, I think I would have given in to depression. Unfortunately, great friends cannot take the place of a wife. I stayed as busy as I could, but late at night it was impossible to avoid the truth that I was alone. I remember calling my parents one evening and crying on the phone about how lonely I was. It hurt to confess my loneliness to my parents and to hear my mother's sobs on the other end of the phone. I wanted to protect them from the hurt and pain that I felt, but when there was no one else to talk with, it seemed my parents were the only ones I could call.

Each day I prayed for comfort. I knew healing didn't come quickly after a loss of this depth, but the pain was so intense at times that I begged for some relief. A coteacher and great Christian friend listened patiently to my questions during those early days. I remember asking him, "When will the pain go away? I feel like I will never stop hurting." He had no answers, but he still listened. He was a true friend.

I learned a lot about anger that year. When the shock of my wife's announcement began to fade during the first few days, I began to experience anger like I had never felt before. I felt very conflicted—I both loved and hated my wife. I would diligently work to win her back, and then feel so much anger toward her that I wished she were dead. The more powerless I felt, the more angry I became. I seldom showed that anger to my wife, but when I was alone or with friends, I would lash out or curse. Sometimes I just wanted to scream.

The more powerless I felt, the more angry I became.

I remember a specific situation that made me so angry that I frightened myself. It occurred after the divorce when the judge had established a visitation schedule. I hadn't seen my son for two months because my wife had temporary custody prior to the court ruling. The coming weekend was the first time I would get to see him. On Thursday, my wife called to tell me that she had moved out of state over a hundred miles away. She said I would have to drive up there to see my son for the weekend. When I said that I'd come get him if she would drive to pick him up at my house on Sunday, she said I'd have to wait to see him until the lawyers worked it out and hung up. The situation wasn't fair, and there was nothing I could do about it. I should have been able to walk into the next room to see my son, but now I wouldn't get to see him for another week. My heart began to race, and all I could do was pace back and forth. Then I exploded. I screamed at the top of my lungs for ten minutes. I don't know if there's an official measure determining when anger becomes rage, but I would have feared for my wife's safety had she walked into the house that evening. That was the closest I had ever come to being totally out of control. It served as a valuable lesson to me. No amount of anger would ever right the wrongs I faced. I had to find a different way to deal with the situation.

That different way came very slowly. It began when someone recommended that I read the Psalms. Nowhere else in Scripture do God's people express their feelings with such honesty. The book is known for its beautiful praises, but it is also filled with anger, questions, doubts, and fears—exactly the feelings that I had been experiencing. Each psalm helped me in a unique way, but none more powerfully than Psalm 27.

> The Lord is my light and my salvation—
>   whom shall I fear?

I could make a list of things, people, and possible events that I feared.

> When evil men advance against me
>   to devour my flesh,
> when my enemies and my foes attack me,
>   they will stumble and fall.

You gain a better understanding of what it means to have people devour your flesh when you experience the kind of hurt divorce brings.

> For in the day of trouble
>   he will keep me safe in his dwelling;
> he will hide me in the shelter of his tabernacle
>   and set me high upon a rock.

Oh, how I longed to feel safe and sheltered, but this was my day of trouble, and where was God?

The entire psalm seemed to have been written for me. But the ending blew me away.

> I am still confident of this:
>> I will see the goodness of the Lord
>> in the land of the living.
> Wait for the Lord;
>> be strong and take heart
>> and wait for the Lord.

Was this true? God's goodness will be seen even in this life? Where would I find it? How would I get there? The answer was in Scripture: *"Wait for the Lord."* If Scripture is true, then God's answer to my pain was written on the page I stared at: *"Wait for the Lord."*

For me, this was the test of faith. I had been in church from birth, a Christian since I was nine years old. I had been educated in a Christian high school and trained at a Christian college. All of that had prepared me, but none of it guaranteed my faith. All of my prior faith struggles paled in comparison to this almost insurmountable hurdle. Did I trust God? Everything hinged upon my answer to that question.

Did I trust God? Everything hinged upon my answer to that question.

I have seen friends lose their faith over a failed marriage or the death of a parent or child. I, too, experienced feelings of doubt, wondering where God was when I needed him, asking why he refused to step in and stop this travesty. I felt like Peter did when the great crowds that followed Jesus began to disappear.

As the crowds were leaving, Jesus turned to his twelve chosen disciples and asked if they wanted to leave also. This was their opportunity to fish or cut bait. I identify with Peter's less than enthusiastic answer: "Lord, to whom shall we go?" Do you get the feeling that Peter may have already checked out the options? That sounds like me. I probably would have considered anything that would have relieved my pain and stress. If someone had promised me a healed marriage, I would have bought into whatever they were selling. I believe Jesus' teachings made Peter uncomfortable at times. I believe Peter wondered whether this teacher were going to deliver on his promises. However, Peter was confident about one thing—this Jesus had the words of eternal life. And sometimes that was all Peter had to hold on to.

At the end of the year following the divorce, I found myself at the end of my rope; now the decision facing me was whether I was going to hang on or let go. Letting go looked so attractive, but the ominous command of Psalm 27 echoed inside me: "Wait for the Lord." Giving up would have relieved me of some stress, but the promise of seeing God's goodness again revived my courage. I wasn't strong enough to pull myself back up that rope, but God's command didn't require that. What it required was all I could do: "Be strong and take heart and wait." And that is what I did. I tied a knot at the end of that rope and hung on for dear life—my eyes glued to the horizon awaiting God's action. By waiting on the Lord, I learned some invaluable lessons.

I learned that the only thing the omnipotent God doesn't exercise power over is the human will. Every day I begged God to change my wife's heart, and every day it seemed that she became more committed to her decision to leave. Where was God's power? Why didn't he act?

Paul talked about the dual natures within us—the sinful nature and the spiritual nature. But there is also a third part—self. While self is neither part of the sinful nature nor the spiritual nature, it freely chooses to submit to one or the other, therefore becoming sinful or spiritual. God can stir the spiritual nature and Satan may stir the sinful nature, but ultimately, "self" chooses which one to submit to.

I wasn't strong enough to pull myself back up that rope, but God's command didn't require that.

I found it frustrating and ironic that the more I prayed to God to intervene and open my wife's eyes to the terrible decisions she was making, the more she was determined to leave. At first I questioned whether God were teasing me or really answering my prayers. But as I began to understand free will, I saw that God was indeed acting to answer my prayers. I believe that God stirred my wife's spiritual nature each time I prayed; and each time he did, she was forced to decide which nature she would submit to. God was answering my prayers, but my wife was continuing to choose her sinful nature.

I learned that prayer can bring peace. At first, prayer caused more turmoil than peace because I would pray for changes and then watch to see if God would act. When he didn't respond on my timetable or like I wanted him to, I grew more frustrated with him and began to question whether I should trust such an important matter to this kind of God.

The final straw came when my wife and I stood in the doctor's office together. My wife had said that she would work on our marriage if I could prove that our son was my biological child. The only thing that stood between me and a rescued marriage was a few drops of blood, a lab assistant, and God. I remember praying for a miracle as we drove toward the doctor's office that morning. A God who could change water to wine could surely match up some DNA. This was the time for God to act. We had to wait ten days for the results to come back, and each overflowed with tension.

Jesus' prayer in the garden helped me understand the peace that praying with full trust can bring. In the depths of personal turmoil, Jesus went off alone and pled with God for intervention. "Everything is possible for you," Jesus said in Mark. He knew God had the power. Then came the request: "Take this cup from me." Had that been the end of Jesus' prayer, I don't think he could have gone to the Cross with such determination and confidence. He would have been second-guessing God the whole way, anxiously looking for intervention around every corner. It was Jesus' final statement in this prayer that gave him peace: "Yet, not what I will, but what you will." Jesus' confidence that God would do what was best gave him the courage to go to the Cross. No matter what the outcome, Jesus had faith that God would do what was best.

My prayers suddenly began to bring me peace when I realized that I wasn't responsible for answering my own prayers. I'd be less than honest if I said that I always believed that the events I faced would turn out for my good. My human logic took over often and tried to convince me that God didn't know what he was doing and that I'd better take the wheel. However, every time I took over, I lost that peace. Ironically, it was more comforting to trust God and not know where he was leading me than to try to steer my own course.

It was more comforting to trust God and not know where he was leading me than to try to steer my own course.

I came to a realization on the night before the lab results were to arrive by mail: Blood tests don't alter a father/son relationship, nor do they create love in a broken marriage. If I trusted God to alter DNA, I could also trust him to bless me in spite of DNA. I suddenly felt peace because I understood that God's ability to bless me was not limited by those test results—and I never opened the envelope.

I learned important lessons about the power gained from reading Scripture. As I stated earlier, I found great comfort in reading the Psalms. I can vividly remember that, during those early days, I found it impossible to go for more than a couple of hours without gaining reassurance from God's Word. I took every opportunity to get away with my Bible and quietly soak in the comforting message of protection, guidance, and hope from God's own words. I regret that I don't still feel that desperate need that drove me to Scripture. Of course the need is still there, but the desperation has long passed. Although I study Scripture regularly and still find great comfort from sitting quietly with my Bible, I sometimes believe that I would gladly endure the pain again to enjoy the "holy addiction" I felt towards Scripture during that time.

I learned a valuable object lesson about forgiveness. When we talk about forgiveness, we generally limit it to people who have expressed sorrow for wronging us. From childhood, the lesson was ingrained into our minds: one person says he's sorry; the other forgives him. But in my situation there was no apology, and there was no sorrow. In fact, my wife had finally convinced herself that she was doing the right thing. How could I forgive something like this? Surely, no one would expect it.

I remember praying for her and being unable to ask for anything good. In fact, the only way I could pray for her was to ask that she would get what was coming to her in the Judgment. I felt that, without her apology, any forgiveness I granted would be like giving my approval of her behavior. Every time we were together, I made sure to remind her that what she was doing was wrong. I couldn't love because I was too busy condemning. In my mind, justice had to come before forgiveness; therefore, I could not forgive.

It was Jesus' teachings in the Sermon on the Mount that opened my eyes to a broader understanding of forgiveness. He said if you only love those who love you in return, you're no better than a tax collector. Even the pagans express that kind of love. Jesus said, "Be perfect, therefore, as your heavenly Father is perfect" (Matt. 5:48). However, more than his teachings, Jesus' actions really hammered home the message of true forgiveness. While Jesus hung on the Cross, being executed unjustly for a crime he didn't commit, the crowd that once praised him as Messiah gawked at him and abused him. Had I experienced a similar kind of injustice, I knew what I would have done. What these people deserved was immediate and irrevocable justice. What they got was grace: "Father, forgive them, for they do not know what they are doing." The ones nailing his hands and feet to the Cross were merely pawns in a game orchestrated by Satan. The crowds who spit on this innocent man had been duped. Instead of anger, Jesus felt love and pity and forgiveness.

How could I forgive something like this? Surely, no one would expect it.

That understanding changed me. Once I understood that Satan was the real villain, I was freed from having to hate my wife for her involvement in his destructive plans. I was no longer responsible for bringing about justice, and that freed me to love her, even though she refused to recognize that her actions were hurtful.

Learning to wait for the Lord was a trying lesson, but one that has forever changed me. Through a series of events that can be classified as nothing less than miraculous, I moved to Memphis, Tennessee, where I met and married a beautiful Christian woman. The growth I experienced through this trial motivated me to want to preach, and now I serve a wonderful congregation in southern Illinois. My son and I not only have a continuing relationship, but now he lives with me for most of the year. My ex-wife and I have a good relationship and talk often about the important roles we share as parents. She isn't a Christian, but nothing would excite me more than to see her in heaven. We talk about it occasionally, and I pray about it often.

I tell people that I would never wish this kind of hurt or pain on anyone, but I wouldn't trade the experience for anything in the world. I am who I am today because of my past and because of God's promise that if I will wait for the Lord, I will see his goodness. I am so thankful that I chose to stand firm and am grateful that God was faithful to his words. Since my experience, I seem to attract many who have experienced similar losses. I have talked with several members in our church who have gone through painful divorces, and we recently organized a grief support group for parents who have lost children. Each person's loss is unique, yet each loss is also tremendously similar. Every one of them has felt piercing and unquenchable pain and loneliness. All of them have questioned God and struggled with doubt. No one has escaped the last few inches of the rope and the decision to let go or to hang on.

> I would never wish this kind of hurt or pain on anyone, but I wouldn't trade the experience for anything in the world.

I am astounded by the number of books on the market today to help people survive these types of losses. Each book may approach it from a different angle, but the ones of any true value must finally address the commands and promises of Psalm 27.

Sin, death, loss, and pain are inevitable parts of this life. There is no way to escape them. Our only hope is to stand strong in the face of them. Do we truly believe that in every tragedy, God can still provide goodness to his faithful people? Are we willing to wait on him? I hope that my story will help you trust God's promises more. May it help provide the courage you need to stand strong, to take heart, and to wait for the Lord.

Lisa's STORY

When I think about my divorce, I think about something that happened a long time ago. I was driving home from work one day, and I started thinking about how perfect my life was. I had a wonderful husband, we had just bought a beautiful house, and we were part of a loving church. I felt that nothing bad could happen to us.

But now, when I look back, I see that things were not quite as perfect as they seemed. Mark worked as a paramedic in a nearby town, and his work schedule demanded that he be out of town for two or three days at a time. I didn't like him being away from home at night, but he really liked his job and I tried to be understanding.

Then, when our son, Alex, was born, Mark got a new job where he worked 8 to 5 and was home evenings. I was thrilled! Having him home at night made us seem more like a real family.

And then when Alex started getting frequent ear infections, I really appreciated having Mark around for moral support—I was a first-time mom and a little bit nervous.

But Mark wasn't as happy to be home as I was to have him there. He didn't like dealing with a sick baby, and he didn't like helping a tired wife. When he started talking about going back to his old job, I was hurt and angry. He wanted to be gone, and I wanted him home. This became a real source of tension between us, and we fought about it often.

Mark didn't want to be home. He didn't like dealing with a sick baby, and he didn't like helping a tired wife.

And then one day, he just went back to his old job without telling me. On the Monday before Thanksgiving, he called and informed me that he was back on his old schedule. I was so mad at him for not telling me ahead of time, and I was hurt because this job change implied that he didn't want to be with Alex and me. I just couldn't let it go, and our fighting escalated.

He worked with a single, non-Christian, immoral guy, and since they worked in a small town, they didn't have too many emergency calls. They could do whatever they wanted in between calls, as long as they stayed in their area. He was living the life of single guy while on his work shift; then when he came home, he had the responsibilities of a family—and he didn't like those responsibilities. We began to fight more and more.

We had always gone to church as a family, but Mark started making excuses and finding reasons not to go. When a few of the men from church tried to talk to him, he was friendly and claimed that everything was fine—but it was becoming more and more obvious that things weren't fine. I started talking to him about going to see a marriage counselor, and he eventually agreed—but reluctantly. After only three visits, he refused to go any more. He said it wasn't doing any good.

Pretty soon he started talking about selling our house and moving to the country. We had worked so hard to get our home, and I loved it so much; but finally Mark convinced me it would be better for us to live in the country where we would have more room—he said it would be a great place for Alex to grow up. I began to think that maybe this was a a good sign—maybe he was more committed to our family than I had thought. Perhaps he was finally willing to invest in our family and our long-term future.

We put our house up for sale, but things between Mark and me continued to get worse. We fought all the time and about everything. Many of our worst fights revolved around his work schedule and his unwillingness to be home. I knew he wasn't happy, but I didn't know why. It became more and more obvious that he didn't want to be home even the little time he was. If I was home, he'd find something else to do and leave. When I tried to talk to him about our growing distance and his obvious unhappiness, he'd just sit there and look at me. His most frequent input to the conversation was, "I just don't know what you want me to say, Lisa." That was it.

He was gone more and more, and without explanation. Sometimes he would go "jogging" and be gone for hours. I began to suspect that he might be having an affair, but I refused to really believe it, and I didn't confront him because that might make it real—and I didn't want it to be real.

Mark took a new job working fewer hours and bringing home less money. With him working less, we began to have some serious financial problems. We had agreed that I would work only part time after Alex was born. I worked as a nurse and would get up very early so I could work the morning shift and be home with Alex in the afternoons. But as our finances got tighter, he began to blame me for our difficulties. He said if I weren't so lazy and would work more hours, we could get out of debt. So I started working full time. It broke my heart to have to leave Alex so much.

Soon after that, our house sold, and we prepared to move into an apartment until we could start building our new home. Mark began asking a lot of questions about our bills and how much we owed and how much money we made in the sale of the house. I had always taken care of all the financial matters in our family, and Mark had never shown any interest in anything to do with money. His sudden interest really puzzled me.

Eventually, we got everything moved into the new apartment. The day after the sale on the house closed, Mark got the last of our things moved into the apartment. When I came home from work that first day in the apartment, Mark was gone. I found a note on the table saying we didn't love each other anymore and that we would be better off if we separated. How could he say that "we" didn't love each other any more! How could he say "we" would be better off separated! I knew that we fought a lot, but I still loved him very much, and there was no way that a separation was good for any of us. This was not the way it was supposed to be!

I called a good friend from church, and she and her husband came right over. My sweet friend made all the necessary phone calls, while her husband tried to take care of Alex. I cried the rest of the night; I didn't know I had so many tears in me.

From the moment I read that awful note, I felt absolutely lost. I cried all the time. For the next couple of weeks, someone from church was with me every minute of the day. Friends took turns staying the night with me or I would stay the night with them. I just didn't feel I could be alone. I don't know what I would have done without them.

I felt absolutely lost. I cried all the time.

It soon became obvious that Mark had been planning to leave ever since he suggested we sell our house. He never did intend for us to build a house in the country—that was just a ploy to get our house sold. He only spent three nights in the apartment that he had insisted we move into.

While we were moving into the apartment, Mark had been putting all sorts of things in storage. It made sense to put some things in storage since we were moving into a smaller living space; so I didn't pay too much attention to what he was moving or where. I assumed it would all end up in our new house someday. But, in reality, he'd been putting all of his personal things in storage, little by little—and anything else he wanted.

Some of the men from church tried again to talk with Mark, but he was very uncommunicative and evasive. He just didn't want to deal with it.

Even though Alex was only fifteen months old, he knew something was wrong. He began to get clingy, and he cried if I tried to leave him anywhere. I know he felt the turmoil.

Mark moved to a town a few hours from us to train for a new job and had an affair while there. He eventually moved back to the town I lived in and soon moved in with a new girlfriend. Mark did show some interest in seeing Alex on a regular basis, and for this I was glad. Alex missed his daddy and needed to spend time with him, but I didn't want Alex to be with Mark's girlfriend. Mark agreed he wouldn't take Alex around her—but it was hard to believe that he'd do what he said.

I would have taken him back for a long time after he left—longer than most people knew.

In spite of all Mark had done, I desperately wanted us to get back together. I tried to talk to him, but he would just sit there and listen. "I just don't know what you want me to say to you, Lisa," is all he would say. I would have taken him back for a long time after he left—longer than most people knew. It always upset me to see him. I finally began asking friends from church to be with me when Mark came to the apartment to pick up and drop off Alex.

My church family continued to be my support. They helped with Alex, and there was always someone I could call when I was upset. I learned how important the simplest expressions of love can be. Sympathetic hugs and a caring "How are you doing?" gave me so much comfort. Receiving a hug without having to talk about everything made me feel loved and accepted. Just knowing that people were praying for me gave me strength.

The surprising thing about the breakup of our marriage was how much it *hurt*. It hurt knowing he was with another woman; it hurt knowing he was going on with his life. I couldn't understand how he could leave Alex, and when I asked him about it, he said he didn't leave Alex, he only left me. But that's not true. He left his son. How could he only see him a couple days a week?

For a long time, I felt like I would never stop crying, and I thought I would always want him to come back. I prayed constantly that he would come back to us, and I really believed that he would. I believed God would bring him back because that's what I wanted.

I believed God would bring him back because that's what I wanted.

But after one of the elders from church talked to Mark, he told me that Mark was going to file for divorce. Mark never did tell me himself; he just went to lawyer and filed the papers. I came home from work one night and found a note on my door from the sheriff, who had come by trying to serve papers. When

I later asked Mark why he hadn't had the decency to tell me him-self, he said he didn't think he needed to tell me—he thought I knew. But I didn't know. I didn't want to know. I didn't want it to be true.

At first I continued praying that Mark would come back to me, even though down deep I knew he wouldn't. Then I went through a time when sometimes I prayed he would come back, and sometimes not. Eventually, I realized that Mark's way of life was not best for me or Alex and that God would take care of us without Mark. I finally know that we are better off without him. I still pray that Mark will come back to God, but even if he does, I know we won't get back together.

It's been a year and a half since Mark left, and I've learned some valuable lessons from my experience. *I'm learning what it means to follow God.* I used to hear people talk about "following God," and I didn't know what they meant. Now I'm beginning to learn.

I'm learning to rely on God and allow him time to work things out in my life. I used to try to fix things myself—especially, when I was still hoping that Mark and I would get back together. I would arrange for people to talk to him and try to convince him to come back to me. But, now, I've finally let that go. I know God is with me and that he will take care of me.

I'm learning the value of prayer. God has answered so many of my prayers. One specific answered prayer sticks out in my mind. When I go to visit my Dad, I have to drive by the trailer where Mark lived while working as a paramedic. The first time I made that trip after Mark left, it just tore me up to see that trailer. I felt so much pain. I prayed for peace, and all of a sudden I stopped crying. I drove the rest of the way to my dad's house in peace. God gave me peace for that moment.

God gave me peace for that moment.

I've also learned to rely on other people. Before this experience, it had always been hard for me to talk to people about my problems, but since all this happened, I've opened up more and have gotten closer to so many loving people.

While I've learned some lessons, I still struggle with some things. I'm trying to learn not to hate Mark's live-in girlfriend. A Bible class teacher recently said that it's wrong for Christians to hate anybody. I immediately thought, "I hate her." After class, I asked the teacher if there was ever a time when it was okay for Christians to hate. He told me to hate what the person is doing, but don't hate the person. I'm working on it, but I can't say I've gotten to that point yet. Sometimes I even hate Mark.

And I struggle with Alex's visitations to Mark. I want Alex to see Mark—he needs to see his dad—but sometimes Mark tries to change the schedule at the last minute and then gets mad at me if I can't change my schedule to fit his new demands. And I worry when Alex is with Mark, because I know Mark sometimes has him in environments that aren't good for him. Mark promises he won't take Alex where there's drinking, but I don't trust him.

Sometimes I'm resentful toward Mark when my life gets extra hectic. When I get sick, I'm angry that he's not there to help me. When I have to be at work at 5:30 in the morning, I'm angry that Mark's not there to take care of Alex—it's hard to find someone to keep him that early. If Mark were still with us, I wouldn't have these problems.

And I get worried when I think about Alex having to grow up without a father at home. There will be lots of times when he needs a daddy—and his daddy won't be there. I grew up without a father in my home, and I know how much that impacted me. I worry that it will impact Alex even more since he's a boy.

And I worry about how I will explain Mark's behavior to Alex when he gets older. How will I explain to Alex that things his dad does aren't right? What will I say to him when he asks what happened and why?

The whole prospect of being a single mom scares me.

The whole prospect of being a single mom scares me. I constantly pray that God will give me wisdom to raise Alex to be a Christian man, that I'll know the right things to say, and that I'll discipline him right. I worry that I'm too hard on him or too easy on him. I pray about it a lot.

Through all of this, I have learned that God is faithful, that I can count on him no matter what. He has been with me every step of the way, and I know, without a doubt, that he will continue walking right beside me for the duration.

STORY THREE

Phil's STORY

"It is therefore ordered, adjudged, and decreed by this court that the bonds of matrimony heretofore existing by and between Petitioner and Respondent be, and the same hereby are, dissolved and terminated."

In other words, I was now divorced. That "Decree of Dissolution" was finalized on March 1, 1990. Even now, I don't know all the reasons. I'm sure I never will. How could a marriage filled with love and hope for the future end with a legal document where husband and wife are described as "Petitioner" and "Respondent"? What was worse, how could one of them be me? It was never supposed to be that way.

In early 1988, at thirty-one years of age, I was surely on my way to something great. Having gone to college on an ROTC scholarship, I had been in the regular Army for seven years. Though medically discharged, I simply viewed that as an open door for an amazing civilian career. My wife held an accounting degree and worked for an investment company, with potential for earnings in the six-figure range. I was employed by a security company contracted to provide security on a college campus. I served as the campus security director and loved every challenging minute of it. I put my graduate degree in management to good use. It was working. I preached the philosophy; the officers carried it out. The university seemed impressed with our service, and I just knew any day they would hire me directly, triple my salary, and I would take another step toward the top of my profession.

Sue and I lived in the farming country outside of Indianapolis, a city with opportunities, yet without many of the large-city problems. We had a brick, three-bedroom, ranch-style home with a large yard and open spaces front and rear. We had taken our graduate courses together (every class), so I dreamed of great opportunities as we each pursued careers. I often thought of my college buddies who, for some odd reason, had tried to talk me out of marrying the girl I loved. Ten years had passed. I was proud to have proved them wrong.

I also believed we were in the right spot spiritually. As a college student, I had preached regularly for a small church in the Missouri boot heel. Throughout my military career, I preached whenever and wherever I was asked. In all those places, I also taught Bible classes, usually adults. I never let my career interfere with my church work. Only in the most dire circumstances would I ever miss worship. My reputation in the local church was one of trustworthiness and stability.

So there we were. Everything seemed on track. So far, we were doing life pretty well. Except for a few rough spots (as all marriages have, I reasoned), we had done everything correctly. We waited until after graduating from college to marry. We had similar economic, religious, and educational backgrounds. We could talk about world events or what to have for dinner with equal comfort. We even voted the same way (I think). But in the latter half of January 1988, things began to change. I should have seen the storm clouds gathering, but I never looked.

The first evidence of serious problems came after Christmas. It began when Sue started staying out late at night. I knew little about where she was or whom she was with. This continued until I came home one Sunday evening from church to an empty house. I knew she wouldn't be home that night when I checked the bathroom and saw that her toothbrush was gone. She stayed away for six weeks. All I could learn was that she was terribly unhappy. I was so ill-equipped to handle this that I made things worse by insisting on answers each time we talked. When would she come home? Why did she leave? She didn't know. Finally, she returned in time for a visit from my parents. For the next several months, I tried to figure out how to solve the problem. I assumed this was my duty, but I had few clues about what was wrong. My problem-solving skills were good in business, but they weren't worth much in my marriage. I didn't try another approach until I finally located a woman who was a Christian professional counselor. After some persuasion, I convinced Sue we should go talk to her.

In October, we began regular counseling sessions. To decrease the tension in our home and to allow emotions to remain calm, I moved into an efficiency apartment closer to the campus where I worked. At the time, I had no idea that I would never live in our house again. My intent was that we would fix our marriage.

I felt somewhat like a failure for having to get outside help, but, if that's what it took, we would do it.

I came home one Sunday evening from church to an empty house. She stayed away for six weeks.

For the next several months, we met and went over everything. The counselor was well trained and very methodical. She dealt with each issue as it emerged. She got one side of the story, then turned to the other and got the response. She chastised each of us, in turn, for our lack of communication. That was probably our greatest fault. How could two people with no children and so much in common talk so little? The sessions were a painful but valuable experience for me. I learned a great deal and wanted to go home and make a go of the marriage again.

The time came when the counselor said she thought we had worked through everything that seemed to be an obstacle. We must now put into practice the things we had discussed, and the only way to do that was for me to move back into the house. I agreed; I was ready. But there was one problem. Sue wasn't ready. She could see nothing different. No amount of talking could convince her that she would be any happier.

We ended the counseling no closer together than when we began. In fact, geographically, we were now ten miles apart. There were deeper issues that we obviously never touched. Our lives were in limbo. I was paying rent on an apartment and mortgage on a house, plus all the other bills. After several more months, I decided on a risky move. I filed for divorce, with the single intent of moving us off center. I hoped it would convince Sue that the situation was serious and that neither of us could continue being so physically and emotionally distant. I had no intention of allowing it to become final.

During the next few months, I offered several times to stop the process if I could get some idea of when we might be able to live in the same house again. I never did. I could have moved back home and let her be the one to leave (she said if I did, she would), but that would have served no purpose. I wasn't concerned about the technicality of "who moved out." Our preacher tried his hand at counseling with us. During those two months, the sessions became more intense and less productive. He did the best he could. He simply got in too late in the game, and we were too far behind.

Eventually, we agreed on property division. There were no legal obstacles, but I was unwilling to hurry the situation along. The marriage was long dead; all that remained was the official funeral. Though I was miserable, I wasn't anxious for it to happen. The divorce became final the first day of March 1990, after I told my attorney to just finish it. The twenty-six-month ordeal was over, but the aftermath remained. The storm had done much damage. Inside I was a mess.

During the process of my divorce, I spent most of my time asking, *Why?* I second-guessed everything, all the way back to my wedding. What could I have missed? Some people said, "It was just a marriage that shouldn't have happened." I disagree! It's true that some marriages shouldn't take place, but I don't believe my marriage was a mistake. The mistakes came later. Because I now realized our mistakes, I was overwhelmed with feelings of failure. This bothered me more than the personal rejection.

I once had all the answers—religious and secular. Now, I knew nothing for sure. I had been so certain that divorce couldn't happen to me. Now, anything could happen, and I felt powerless to control any of it. I was a manager, but I hadn't been able to manage my marriage. At the office, my coworkers sometimes came to me with personal problems concerning relationships. There was a time when I was comfortable offering sage advice on such things. But now I felt contagious and didn't want to spread the disease further. "You're asking the wrong person," I'd tell them. The storm had done a number on my confidence.

Sometimes I just cried. Divorce is sad. The demise of a marriage is a very real death for those involved. Marriage is a living entity in that it identifies and defines a person. I noticed all the couples at any gathering. I wasn't part of a couple any longer. I was now a statistic. I hated the thought of being part of that disturbing number of marriages that had failed (the ones you hear about from the pulpit), yet I was now included. My family invited me to come live with them and look for work. I couldn't do it. That would be too much like flunking college and coming back home to start all over. Though I had flunked marriage, I couldn't go home to start over.

I wasn't part of a couple any longer. I was now a statistic.

There is a difference in being alone and in being lonely. Sometime I was just alone. I read some really large books during my spare time, which was plentiful. Often while reading, I found myself staring at the wall, not knowing how long I had been doing so. I kept hoping this bad dream would end. I had to adjust to being with just me. Other than my job, my schedule was totally mine, but that got old quickly. Sure, I could go to a movie at a moment's notice, but seeing all those movies alone turned into loneliness. Meals were lonely. I had no idea meals were such a social event. Eating alone, whether at home or out, was much too quick. It became a task instead of an enjoyable event. As a result, my weight dropped noticeably, along with my confidence.

I had to adjust to being with just me.

I spent more hours at work for no reason. I wasn't anxious to get to a tiny, empty apartment. After a few weeks of just hanging around after normal hours, I began getting hints from my shift supervisors to go home. Even they didn't need me. It seems I had been too successful in accomplishing my goal of setting up the department to run without me. Once I was sick for three days and stayed in bed. I called in, expecting to solve problems on the phone. I was told by my right-hand man that everything was going great. He seemed to enjoy it too much. What else could I expect? It's what I had set out to do. Even the thing that was successful didn't feel that way.

On the positive side, since I had so much free time, I thought that maybe I could become a missionary. They probably hadn't heard about my divorce in India. I could just go there and work all the hours I wanted. I didn't take this thought seriously, but it was a possibility. I tried hard not to fall into a self-imposed exile, but the tendency was there at times. Meanwhile, I learned about ministries I never knew existed, such as a group called "Overcomers" at another church in town. I found empathy and support at their devotionals, and the group went on outings that helped a great deal. Most of all, these widows, widowers, and divorced men and women were finding ways to serve God. Some churches do their best not to lose divorced or abused people.

Then, around Christmas in 1989, I met Vicki. I had known her parents for years and had heard of the tragic death of her husband. The accident had occurred about the same time my home began to crumble.

The very thought of meeting someone else scared me. Every book I had read advised the newly divorced not to look for a new relationship for at least a year. (I still believe that's sound advice.) So I didn't look for one. A new relationship was the last thing on my mind. I had resigned myself to the probability of being single for the rest of my life. But Vicki seemed to be at every church function, along with her blonde-haired, dimpled, nearly two-year-old son.

I was a bit concerned when we started spending more and more time together. I told her so in one of our many long phone conversations. She agreed, yet didn't seem worried. We spent hours talking about everything we had been through. As time passed, it became obvious that we were being led by a Presence larger than ourselves. Against advice to wait, we were married on March 10, 1990. I instantly had a son, and it was obvious that he felt it was his job to initiate me into the joys of parenting a two-year-old! A year and half later, we presented him with a little sister—my first offspring! Together they make a constantly joyous, constantly challenging combination that requires all my resources.

Several months before I met Vicki I had strongly perceived that I was on the verge of something important—something good. Even with the pending divorce, I anticipated the future. I was sure it would be career related. I thought an opportunity would soon appear, and I was ready to step through an open door to bigger money and greater responsibility. But that wasn't it at all. I now believe that the "something important" was a family and a new life. I never saw those possibilities. Only God could have known. Only he could have put this family together so quickly.

How do I know he did it? The context of our meeting (at church) and the context of our talks (serving him) convinced me. Our first desire was to serve God, whether as singles or together. I hadn't known such openness before. The difference between this marriage and my first was that in my first I strictly relied on my own judgment.

Now I trust God to lead my life. My perspective about who is in control changed.

I could never have planned the life I now have. Vicki supported my desire to go into full-time ministry, and we are now involved with a church family that is warm, loving, prayerful, and supportive.

I learned a number of things from my divorce. *I learned never to blame God or flee from his people.* My divorce was not his fault, nor theirs. In fact, God made the pain bearable. He always does.

I learned about love and support in time of need from people who demonstrated it. A brother caught me by the shirtsleeve one evening in the church building, pulled me into a classroom, and looked me straight in the eye. He said, "Brother, I know what you're going through. I've been through it myself, and if you ever want to talk, you let me know." That's all he said. I never took him up on it, but knowing he would be there was the backup I needed at the time. (Thanks, Alex.) A Christian sister who had been through a divorce supplied me with books. First, I read a set on how to keep your marriage together. Then, when it seemed to be a loss, she gave me more books on how to survive a divorce. I had plenty of time to read, and I gained something from each book. I experienced many other such acts of kindness and words of encouragement.

I learned that I must take responsibility for my part in the divorce—but no more. Another person made decisions over which I had no control.

I have learned (in both marriages) that no one comes into marriage empty-handed. In fact, a person comes with a full load of baggage from family, personal experience, temperament, environment, and religion. Your spouse's model of family may be the same as yours, or it may be different. Without a lot of communication and awareness, the smallest infraction can be magnified into a major problem.

I learned that there are no guarantees for a permanent marriage. In fact, Satan and his forces attack Christian marriages with full force because such homes are where God's people flourish.

I learned that God forgives divorced people. It's humans who have a difficult time with it. Prior to my divorce, I probably would have reacted negatively toward someone who was divorced. God carved away a large chunk of my ego in teaching me this lesson. Along the bumpy road of divorce, I lost the urge to set everyone straight. I hope I never get it back.

Along the bumpy road of divorce, I lost the urge to set everyone straight. I hope I never get it back.

I have now learned that the pain will come back if you write it all down for everyone to read. But, if you've found something worthwhile in my mess, it's been worth the pain of remembering.

In addition to the lessons I've learned, I'd like to share some suggestions for those going through similar pains.

Keep God involved. Pray, seek his will, and don't let anyone come between you and him. I picked up a particular phrase in one of the books I read where the author likened the crisis to walking into a strong wind (I could feel it). He said to "lean into it" and keep going. It's one of those phrases I still use regularly. You will find particular concepts and phrases that work for you. Use them.

Make the effort to save the marriage. If you succeed, it will be worth it. If you don't, you will learn much in the process. Whatever happens, it will be important to you later to know that you didn't give up easily. Throughout my ordeal, I knew that whatever I did would accompany me my whole life. I would always live with my decisions and efforts (or lack thereof). I had to know I didn't give up easily.

Find someone you can trust and with whom you can talk. I don't believe it's necessary for that person to be divorced, but there are advantages. I found I talked deeply with several people, including those with whom I worked. Some had been divorced; others had not. I found myself apologizing to them for unloading my burdens, but they each said, "No problem." I'll always remember their patience.

When you find yourself walking into a strong wind, lean into it and keep going.

Be aware of and allow for a certain amount of depression as the process continues. You will likely need more rest. I became convinced at one point that I had a terminal disease because of my constant tiredness and one or two other symptoms that could have been related to anything. Only later did I realize that depression manifests itself in physical ways as well as mental and emotional.

Look for what God will do with your crisis. He will make something good from it. Learn to wait for him. If you could solve your own problems, you wouldn't need books like this. Keep leaning into the wind until it lets up; then you will be able to walk straighter than ever before. I believe with all my being that without the wilderness temptation, the human Jesus couldn't have survived Gethsemane. God knew what he was doing then, and he knows now. God bless you.

Jan's STORY

We had been married twenty-six and a half years when he didn't want to be married any longer. We had a wonderful marriage, or so I thought. He was a wonderful, considerate, loving, generous husband and father. We always verbalized "I love you," during or at the close of every phone conversation and each physical parting. We were both Christians and had always been very involved in the church wherever we lived.

I had realized for some months that my normally quiet husband was becoming withdrawn and even quieter. I knew there was a cause and began praying for wisdom, enlightenment, and help. Out of fear that I didn't know what it was or how to help, I asked him to agree to go with me to get some counseling. He agreed. During the months that we counseled with a minister in our area (who had a degree in marriage and family counseling), neither the counselor nor I ever heard any indication that Greg wanted an end to the marriage.

Greg left on Friday, April 21, 1989, and I began the most painful storm of my life. That simple statement does not even begin to convey the unimaginable pain and devastation that separation and divorce carries with it. Only those who have been through it know, and they certainly never want anyone else to know it.

In the beginning, I just could not believe it was happening to me. It wasn't supposed to be this way. I never, in all the years we were married, ever thought that we would not live as husband and wife "till death us did part." I cried a lot. I didn't sleep more than two or three hours each night. I had to make a conscious effort to remember to eat something on a daily basis. I had never known a person could physically hurt as badly as I did yet have no physical injuries. I didn't feel like I would live, yet at the same time I was afraid I would.

I didn't feel like I would live, yet at the same time I was afraid I would.

I love and serve a loving, kind, wonderful, good God. At no time in my pain and depression did I ever feel it was his fault. I did not rail at him with, "Why, God?" In the first few days I could not pray, but I did not feel that what was happening was God's fault. I knew that there is truth in the statement that it takes two to make a marriage, and it takes two to break one. I felt like such a failure. I felt as if I must have been so very blind, since I hadn't seen it coming. I remember feeling like an old shoe that has been tossed aside—no longer needed or wanted.

I felt like an old shoe that has been tossed aside—no longer needed or wanted.

But God reached out and touched me in a very special way. Less than two weeks after Greg left, I decided to open a checking account in my name alone. At the bank where I applied for a checking account the clerk told me that if I would apply for a credit card with their bank that my first order of checks would be free. "Well," I thought, "I'll apply, but I know I won't get it. But, then, free checks are free checks." You see, less than two years prior my husband and I had been forced to file bankruptcy, so I knew I would not get a credit card. Some ten days later I received a Mastercard in the mail with a credit limit of $500. No one but my Father in heaven will ever know the volumes of love that little card spoke to me. Very clearly, I got the message, "I am still in charge. I will take care of you." In the midst of my pain and anguish, God was letting me know that he was going to take care of me all the way through. I have a much greater appreciation for his faithfulness than I had before this awful storm.

In the early weeks during the worst of the pain and depression, I learned a great deal about the love that God has for us, his created creatures. When my husband walked out, I knew he was also going to walk away from his children and the church. I knew he was making a very bad choice. I began to understand that God created us with the freedom to *choose*. He allows us to choose, and then allows us to live with the consequences of the choices made. Before Adam and Eve's first wrong choice, God knew that humans all through time would make wrong choices. Yet he loved us enough to give us the freedom of choice. That may sound like a contradictory statement. If he loved us so much, why didn't he just make us like robots, with no choice? Because, without freedom of choice, we could never experience love, joy, peace, or any of the emotions that are associated with having done what is good and right. I know that it hurts him terribly when we make choices that bring us pain and sorrow, yet he continues to love us and to patiently wait for us to learn the truth of his love.

I could not stand to listen to music.

I remember that I could not stand to listen to music. It seemed that the subject of every song on the radio was love—either how wonderful love is or the pain of love gone sour. I could not bear it. I kept my car radio tuned to a Christian station, where much of the programming was talk radio. The messages I heard often spoke to my heart. Our faithful and loving God fed my soul and carried me, even though I wasn't aware of it at the time.

I was one of the more blessed people on earth. Besides having a very real faith, I had several friends that I refer to as heart friends. What a wonderful blessing they were to me. One sat with me early one morning over coffee and cried with me and told me she would take my pain if she could. And I knew that she meant it.

Because I've endured the storm of divorce, I've learned to be more aware of those around me who are hurting. Now, when someone else goes through a fiery trial or violent storm, I try to find ways to reach out and words to convey that I care and want to help. I also learned some things not to say. Don't say to someone in the middle of the storm, "Time heals all wounds; you'll be okay." I didn't feel like I would be okay, and I didn't want anyone telling me I would be. Also, please don't ever say, "I know how you feel," if you haven't been through the trial. You don't know how it feels if you haven't been there. Instead, say honestly, "I don't know what you're feeling, but I care about you, and I really do want to help."

I remember thinking that I would probably never smile again, much less laugh. I really thought that I was going to have to *endure* the rest of life. But God has told us, in his written Word, that we are to live one day at a time. Here I was, thinking about the rest of life, when I couldn't even handle the evil of the day. Little by little, I began to hear what he was saying to me through his teachings.

I was given a book by Kay Arthur, titled *Lord, Heal My Hurts.* That was a definite turning point for me. As I began to read that book and study the Scriptures found in it, I learned that I must decide that I wanted to be healed. I made that decision and I surrendered everything to God. I told him that with his help I would try to live one day at a time and that I would remember to give my life to him at the beginning of each day. That book was given to me some eight months after my storm began. I am positive that God's timing is perfect. He knew when I would be ready to receive that material. He is so faithful. He is so good. He is worthy. All praise and glory and honor belong to him forever and ever.

I would go through it again, rather than not learn those precious lessons.

I can tell you truthfully that I would not want to experience that kind of pain again. However, that is what it took for me to learn some of the lessons that I have come to understand; therefore, I would go through it again, rather than not learn those precious lessons. Like I said, I already possessed a real faith, but now I have a much closer relationship with my Father. I am learning to know him—not just about him—and knowing him is the most wonderful thing that has ever happened to me.

Ben's STORY

For thirty-four years of what I perceived to be a good, though imperfect, marriage, divorce was never contemplated. Though our culture has long been "in the throes" of this social plague, it was anathema to me. As far as I was concerned, I was living in the best of all possible worlds—considering the circumstances of my health—and naively believed that my marriage would last "until death us did part." Additionally, after being a minister for seventeen years, I believed and sought to practice what I preached.

For all but six years of our marriage, I lived with a debilitating chronic health condition. This, of course, had taken its toll on the quality of our lives. It was always clear to me that my condition weighed more heavily on my wife's mind than it did on mine. It seemed the "security blanket" that I represented had been taken from her. I deeply regretted this for her sake, but the

Lord enabled me to "keep on keepin' on." I had always tried to reassure her, "Honey, the Lord has provided adequately for us, and I am sure he always will." And, because I trusted her explicitly, I neither saw—nor anticipated—any storm clouds on the horizon of our marriage . . . but they loomed ominously ahead!

Our sons had obtained professional degrees that included time at Christian universities, and our daughter had attained her "MRS" degree in such an environment. And now, five grandchildren later, I was devastated to learn that Satan had intervened in my marriage.

His tool of intervention was a neighbor and acquaintance whom we had known for eight years. A local businessman and an avid hunter and fisherman some ten years my senior (making him eighteen years older than my wife), he became deviously entwined in our lives. The fact that he frequently shared his fish and game with us was no cause for alarm. His visits to our front door were frequent, but mostly very brief. Bob assisted me with chores that I was physically unable to do. He was always quick to volunteer his services.

He learned of our yearly attendance at the local rodeo and invited us to be his guests at the rodeo on two or three different occasions. Because Bob enjoyed cooking, he invited us to have a Thanksgiving and Christmas dinner in his home. Additionally, he invited us to spend a day with him at his beautiful mountain cabin retreat where we enjoyed a delicious cookout. We appreciated and accepted his invitations because we were geographically isolated from our children and other family members on most holidays. He also took us out for dinner on several occasions. I didn't always desire his gratuities, but agreed to go along in order to pacify my wife's legitimate desire for more activity.

Once, we accompanied Bob and a lady friend to a local restaurant for dinner. During the course of our time together, I perceived that they were living together in another town where his business was located. He also maintained a residence in our town, without his "friend." That evening I discussed the matter with my wife, stating that we should no longer accept social invitations from him for conscience's sake. A week later, she informed me that she had spoken to Bob about "my problem," and he had assured her that "it would never happen again."

Satan's tool of intervention was a neighbor and acquaintance whom we had known for eight years.

We spoke to Bob about church from the beginning of our acquaintance. He told us of his membership and regular attendance at a local church. His language and actions never betrayed the truth about what I eventually learned about his "womanizing" reputation—one that long preceded our acquaintance with him. He had been married twice and had children almost my wife's age. But Satan had set us up and was yet to work out his scheme to "break asunder" our marriage.

During the latter months of our marriage, my wife had requested that we move to Las Cruces, New Mexico. This move would put us near one of our children and some of our grandchildren, which seemed a wise choice since our senior years were approaching. I never once hesitated over my wife's request. I had even told several of our friends of our intentions. Developing circumstances revealed that this move was merely the ploy of my betraying wife and her new paramour to further their scheme to remove me from her presence.

According to "our" plan, we went to our son's home some seven hundred miles away in March, 1994. We were there for three days and spent our time looking for houses. Then I left without my wife, as planned, to visit an aged uncle in Dallas before going to visit my mother in Oklahoma. I had planned a two-week stay there before picking up my wife and returning to Colorado. I had been at my mother's for nearly two weeks when a UPS vehicle delivered the most devastating message I could have ever imagined! It read matter-of-factly: "You might as well sit down to read this. I have decided that I am going to divorce you. I have returned home, but will be gone when you arrive. I will be living alone in Grand Junction and will be traveling from time to time to visit the kids and my mother in Sacramento. Don't waste your time trying to locate me." To say that I was totally dumbfounded is an understatement. I was paralyzed!

Divorce was a juggernaut I could never have anticipated. It was contrary to all that I had believed in, preached about, and expected in our marriage. In total amazement at the turn of events, I found no answers for the ordeal that faced me. It couldn't be real—it must be a bad dream!

"No, dear God!" I prayed, "How can it be so? I truly believed our future held greater possibilities for happiness and contentment and less pain. Why, Oh why is this happening at a time when both of us need each other more than ever? Our children and grandchildren need us together. That's the way it has always been; and that it is the way it was meant to be." Oh how desperately I prayed, but in my consternation, I still waited to awake from a horrible nightmare!

Then on April 20, 1994, the process server delivered the papers, officially notifying me of the divorce action initiated by my wife and aided by her new consort and his attorney. There was also a restraining order that declared me to be a violent-tempered person, among other things, and prohibited my having contact with my wife. (In truth, I had never laid a hand on my wife during our marriage except in a tender way, and I had no temper problems.)

The pain that initially engulfed my world has been numbed with the passage of time, but the perplexity lingers. It would have been much easier to have lost my wife in death. Death would have been less painful to endure, less shattering to my ego, more acceptable to live with.

The pain that initially engulfed my world has numbed with the passage of time, but the perplexity lingers.

My thoughts are more rational now than when I first received news of the divorce. It's difficult to believe that I was able to make the necessary decisions regarding the division of our jointly owned property. Certainly my attorney earned her fee by dealing with a "basket case." Packing to move to my present home, located approximately 1,000 miles from "our home," was far less than easy. I remember my unmarried son's lament, "Now, I don't have any place to call 'home.' "

I thought, "Neither do I." But circumstances have forced me to accept the fact that, as a child of God, I have always been just a "poor wayfaring stranger, awaiting a city whose builder and maker is God." Thank God there is something better ahead for me!

Divorce was contrary to all that I had believed in and expected in our marriage.

The pain, embarrassment, tears, and multitudinous emotions that have accompanied my days to this point are bearable only with my Lord's help. My constant emotion echoes the Lord's: I hate divorce! Yes, it takes two people to make a marriage work. I have failed, and it hasn't been easy to live with such a reality. Many things could have been better, but I was reasonably happy and thought she was too. I tried to fulfill my role as a husband to the woman whom I have always loved so very much. However, she would have been quick to declare, "You display your love inadequately." I will readily admit that it wasn't always natural for me to display my affection to my wife's satisfaction, but our relationship had worked for a long time—only to be crumbled by another man! That is the dilemma that continually occupies my thoughts.

I can only thank God that my children were grown and away from home when this happened, and I am thankful that they are all faithful Christians. One of them recently told me, "Dad, we kids will never be happy until you and Mom are together again." Though my son's sentiment was encouraging, I have had to admit to myself that my adversary presently has the upper hand. He has total control of my former wife's life. People who had known her for years were dismayed by her conduct, and all have been supportive with their prayers and numerous expressions of concern.

I understand the apostle's lament when he wrote, "Demas has forsaken me, having loved the present world." My wife's love for this world and what it offers has seemingly become her driving force. I have perceived that she still has a conscience. Thus, I pray continually that it won't become so hardened that she is unable to repent and return to the Lord.

The pain, embarrassment, tears, and multitudinous emotions that have accompanied my days to this point are bearable only with my Lord's help.

The woman whom I knew and lived with for thirty-four years is ever the object of my prayers, as well as those of family, friends, and brothers and sisters in Christ. Two years before our marriage disintegrated, she was diagnosed as having congestive heart failure. Her health problem contributes to my anxiety over her trapped condition in Satan's snare. Yes, I hate divorce! I live with regret over my imperfection as a husband to the woman I love. That pill is bitter and more difficult to swallow than living with multiple sclerosis for twenty-nine years.

Our marriage was "dissolved" on December 20, 1994, two days after our thirty-fifth wedding anniversary. Relating the story rejuvenates the pain, as do family pictures that are packed away. I weep! But there was and will be a better day . . . thank God! I only wish things were different, but one can't unring a bell.

CHAPTER 4

Voices from the Storm of Illness

⊗

INTRODUCTION

People who were sick flocked to him—some came on their own, others were brought by friends and loved ones. And Jesus healed them. Jesus' compassion for the sick—and for their families—is proven over and over by the way he responded to their needs.

> People brought to him all who were ill with various diseases, those suffering severe pain, the demon-possessed, those having seizures, and the paralyzed, and he healed them. (Matt. 4:24)

Introduction

Knowing that God cares about us we when are sick is a source of immense comfort. But knowing that he cares does not eradicate the pain and suffering that prolonged illness brings. The three stories in this chapter each share their experiences with illness from a different viewpoint. Two of our storytellers tell of long-term struggles with cancer—one from the viewpoint of the patient and one from the viewpoint of parents watching the struggle of their son. The third storm-survivor shares seventeen years of watching his wife struggle through a wide variety of ailments and candidly reveals his own personal struggles in dealing with her illness.

Long-term illness wears a family down unlike nothing else. Struggles with finances, struggles with a disrupted life, and struggles with faith are just some of the darts that Satan throws at families experiencing prolonged illness. But in spite of immense pressures and overwhelming demands, these storm survivors held on to their faith in God and he saw them through—no matter the outcome of the illness.

Denis and Kathy's STRUGGLE

"Mrs. Miller, where is your husband? The doctors would like to speak to both of you tonight." This question from the pediatric nurse brought panic and despair to my heart. Our three-year-old son, Adam, had been ill for months with unexplained fevers, bruises, and fatigue. Test after test had revealed nothing, but tonight he lay pale and listless in the hospital crib, desperately ill. My mind flew to Hannah who had begged for a child from the Lord, only to give him back at a very young age. Denis and I had been through the pain of countless miscarriages, surgeries, and heartache. I had been able to carry only one precious child, our daughter Angie, but we had beseeched God for another child, and he had chosen Adam for us to adopt. He was a golden-haired, laughing child from the first, so miraculous to us, so fulfilling to our family, so much fun. He would wait at the door each night, and as soon as he saw his daddy come home, he would say, "Daddy's back. Daddy's back." Denis would lay down on the floor, and Adam would lay down on top of him with a contented sigh, as if his whole world were now safe and complete.

As Denis and I listened in shock and disbelief, the doctors told us that Adam had ALL—acute lymphocytic leukemia, a major killer of young children—that he was acutely ill, and that we had to make plans to leave for St. Jude Hospital in Memphis that evening. I will never forget the nightmare of that night—the helpless feelings, the questions of how this had happened, the guilt of "if only I had caught it earlier," and, most of all, the overwhelming fear.

Immediately, all priorities changed in our lives. Things we had felt were so important—such as home, cars, jobs—became totally insignificant to us. Most of us are unprepared to receive bad news such as this. Somehow we always feel it will happen to someone else or that God will protect us from bad things. Logically, we know that illness and death will come to every person, but when it is your own three-year-old child, the bitter question of *Why?* comes pouring out of your soul. Being raised as a Christian and always doing the "right" thing had in some ways left me with a handed-down religion—young and untested. When something like this happens, all your statements of faith are suddenly on the line. Will you truly trust that God will help you through this, or will you become bitter and curse God?

During the next three years, our faith was refined in fire. Satan sifted us like wheat many times. Sometimes the darkness was overwhelming, and sometimes we felt as if God had abandoned us—our prayers going only as high as the ceiling in the St. Jude's hospital room.

Were we, like Abraham, willing to give up our son if it were God's will? Could we find the blessings in this sorrow to really believe that all things could work for good to those that love the Lord? How could we bear the pain of listening to our child scream during a painful test, "Daddy, don't let them hurt me, don't let them do it! Help me, help me, Daddy"? Would we turn and devour each other because of our anger, helpless feelings, stress, and grief? Would Satan shake our faith, or would we remain unshakable no matter what happened? Could we totally surrender our lives and the life of our son into God's keeping and be thankful in any circumstance?

When your three-year-old child is stricken, the bitter question of *Why?* comes pouring out of your soul.

Writing this has made me cry. Reliving these feelings is painful, and sometimes we are reluctant to dig into painful memories; however, relating to others how God brought us through the storm and holding out hope to them is worth it. I am thankful to say that Adam is now a healthy sixteen-year-old football player, wrestler, and, most importantly, a Christian. He is a living monument to the power of God and the prayers of many.

During a ten-year course, Satan tested us—not only with Adam's leukemia—but in most areas of our lives. I lost my beloved mother and three grandparents between 1977 and 1979.

Adam was diagnosed with leukemia in June 1981. In January 1982 Denis had major back surgery and was off work for six months. The darkness was overwhelming. We became more and more financially troubled and lost our farm, allowing it to return to the original owners instead of declaring bankruptcy. Denis had to have another back surgery and was unable to keep his job as a carpet installer. I am a nurse and care for many AIDS patients. When I cut my finger, I feared contamination and went through many tests to see if I were HIV positive. I wrecked our car. As I look back now, I know that God was the only one carrying us, as the poem "Footprints" states.

One night a man had a dream. He dreamed he was walking along the beach with the Lord. Across the sky flashed scenes from his life. For each scene he noticed two sets of footprints in the sand. One belonged to him, and the other to the Lord.

When the last scene of his life flashed before him, he looked back at the footprints in the sand. He noticed that many times along the path of his life there was only one set of footprints. He also noticed that it happened at the very lowest and saddest times in his life.

This really bothered him and he questioned the Lord about it. "Lord, You said that once I decided to follow you, You'd walk with me all the way. But I have noticed that during the most troublesome times in my life there is only one set of footprints. I don't understand why when I needed You most You would leave me."

The Lord replied, "My precious, precious child. I love you and I would never leave you during your times of trial and suffering. When you see only one set of footprints, it was then that I carried you.

In many ways, our lives mirrored Job's, and we battled anger and depression. Survival was the password—sheer survival, day by day. Hanging on to God was the only way to keep our sanity—that and thinking about all the problems that wouldn't be in heaven like illness, debt, and Satan.

By God's mercy, I am able to say today that God heard our prayers. He cried with us. He held us in his hands during the dark days and kept whispering to us "I am here; I will never forsake you. I will show my unending power and bring you through every trial." He sent us peace in our terror and calm in the night when we couldn't sleep. He strengthened us in our faith. Today, we are all healthy; we have a home and thirteen acres of land. I don't have AIDS, and Denis has an insurance business. I'm glad the farm is gone because we couldn't keep up with the expenses. Our marriage is strong and wonderful. God is so good.

The lessons we learned came hard. Sometimes I ask God if there weren't an easier way to learn them. Maybe not, as we are a stubborn people, somehow always feeling that we will be able to figure things out ourselves instead of depending on God. The following are some of the lessons we learned.

Pray, pray, pray. We asked all of our friends to pray. We had whole congregations praying for us. We called Albert Lemmons in Canada where he was conducting a seminar on prayer and fasting, and he and those who were attending his seminar fasted and prayed for us. Our congregation spent many days in prayer and fasting.

Slow down. Most of the things we work so hard for are materialistic and earthly. I would have given everything I had to make Adam well. In the end, all that matters is your salvation, the salvation of your family, your church family, and winning others to the Lord. Everything else will be given to others when you die, as the rich farmer learned when God called him a fool for storing up treasures on earth.

Pay attention to the important things in life, such as your mate and children. They are the true blessings in life and have been graciously given by the Lord. Make every moment count; don't sweat the little things. Be merciful to your loved ones as God has been merciful to you. Tell them every day what God has done in your life.

Don't take health for granted. We should get down on our knees every morning and thank God for another day to serve him. Don't gripe over petty things.

Take one day at a time. If we had known in the beginning that Adam would go through over fifty bone marrow and spinal taps, or three hundred lab draws and IVs, we would have broken under the knowledge. God will give you the strength necessary for each hour, each minute. Just keep asking for it.

Have a good spiritual foundation in place before the storms come. If the storm doesn't overwhelm you, surviving after it may. Post traumatic shock and depression can last for a long time, and it's difficult to build a spiritual foundation during either the storm or its aftermath. Everyone one of us will face trials at some time. God is interested in how we come through them, how we are refined and tested, if our faith comes out like gold, and whether we turn our backs on him or trust him.

Look for the way the Lord uses others in your life to help ease your journey. Stay alert and notice that he sends others to hold your arms up when you are weary. Learn to lean on others. Denis and I had always been the ones giving others help, and it was hard for us to learn to let others help us. It was always amazing to see how the help came and who God used to bring it. Who can fathom the mind of God or his ways?

Be gracious to those who don't stand by you. One set of friends, who lived four hundred miles away, tracked us down to the hospital in Memphis. It was wonderful to hear their normal, sane voices in the midst of our insanity. But other close friends, not knowing what to say to us, looked in fear at their own healthy children and deserted us. They had not yet been through trials. They didn't know that it didn't matter what they said—I just needed them to come and sit by me, hold my hand, cry with me, tell me a joke. I was the same person I had always been, just lost in a world of hurt. My heart begged friends to please overcome their fear and stay by me.

It didn't matter what they said—I just needed them to come and sit by me.

Don't limit the workings of God. Many Christians feel that miraculous healing ended during the apostolic era, but Denis and I asked our elders to come lay hands on Adam and anoint him with oil. Only one elder and his wife came. They had never done this before and were fearful, but they stepped out in faith and trusted God to do far above what we could ask for. The elder anointed Adam, and we all prayed. It was a beautiful evening; it gave us great peace and comfort and strengthened our faith in God's plan for Christian leaders.

Realize that nonbelievers are watching. They saw us on our knees in the hospital rooms; they saw others ministering to us; they heard us saying, "God is our refuge, in him we will trust." Nonbelievers are affected by how you cope and how you rely on God. A nurse observed, "There are those who don't make it, and then there are those who are prayed for."

Keep life as normal as possible. We came home from the hospital in Memphis one weekend and threw Angie a birthday party. Some asked how we could concentrate on something like that when Adam might be dying. Some normal parts of life must continue; some brightness and laughter help later in the darkness of night. A bright moment during the day gives strength when more bad news comes. Sharing a joke builds strength to fight a little longer. Once, after Adam had had a spinal tap, the doctor said, "We think we see a leukemia cell in Adam's spinal fluid and are afraid he might be relapsing. Please come back in six weeks, and we will know for sure." Living for six long weeks at home without some sort of normality would have been totally unbearable. It was much easier to lift Adam's health up again in prayer and just go on with life at home, trusting in the mercy of God.

Share with others in the same boat. We talked with many other families who had loved ones in St. Jude Hospital, and the bonds we formed helped boost our morale. We shared trips home and back, trips to the hotels, meals, and just plain fellowship. Christians in Memphis were alerted that we were at St. Jude, and they reached out to us.

Absolutely refuse to let Satan win. Speak aloud to him, denounce him, saying, "Anything in this world you throw at me will never make me leave God. I will always belong to God, and he promises me that we will win in the end." Rest in the promises that God will never leave us; believe that he will be there now and through eternity. We may lose our home, but we will always have a place to live. We can lose our jobs, but something else will come up. If I had become HIV positive, God would have given us the strength to get through it, and I would be in heaven where there is no sickness. If Adam had died, life would have gone on in terrible sorrow, but we had the assurance that we would see him again and that we had been blessed by his life for as long as we had him. No matter what trial you are going through, God will work it out for good—not always the way you want, but in God's way. God is greater than anything that Satan can throw at us.

I wouldn't trade what I have learned for anything.

Be assured that in the end you will be able to comfort others with the love God has used to comfort you. You will be able to use the lessons you have learned to help others. I often hear Denis saying, "I wouldn't wish what we have been through on any one, but I wouldn't trade what I have learned for anything." We have counseled, met, and wept with countless parents facing the death of a child through all kinds of illnesses. We are no longer afraid to go sit by them. They need an ear, an arm around their shoulder, a hug. They need to hear someone say, "I understand what you are going through; I've been there myself." God will use your growth to help others, your story of God's amazing grace to encourage them, and your victory to give them hope.

Looking back, I realize how painful things were at times. Our tendency is to do almost anything to relieve the pain—even to the point of denying that we are in pain. Acknowledge the pain. Cry, seek help, ask, and when you don't have answers, just do your best. That's all God expects. The peace we feel is beyond our understanding. It is more than, "Well, the storm is over." It's a peace in which God seems to say, "No matter what, I am there with you, and we will go through this together." His wisdom is beyond understanding, his ways above our ways. He loves us in a way that we can't comprehend. He does carry us beyond the storm to victory. " 'I will turn their mourning into gladness; I will give them comfort and joy instead of sorrow. . . . My people will be filled with my bounty,' declares the Lord" (Jer. 31:13–14).

—Denis and Kathy Miller

Danny's STRUGGLE

On November 29, 1990, my life drastically changed. I had graduated with a bachelor's degree in communications in ministry from a Bible college in Mississippi and had taken a job as minister of a church in Thyatira on July 9, 1989. My ministry was developing, and I was on top of the world. Then something went wrong with some dental treatments. My gums swelled and the swelling wouldn't go down. Dr. Bill Alford, my Christian friend and dentist, ordered me to call my medical doctor for a blood workup.

I went to the hospital that Thursday morning for the blood work. That afternoon my telephone rang just as I was leaving home to go visit a fellow Christian who was dying of cancer. My doctor said, "Danny, you need to get to the hospital and I mean *now!* Your white blood cell count is nine times higher than it should be." He told me to come by his office to pick up some paperwork and then head to Baptist East in Memphis where Dr. Jefferson Upshaw would be waiting for me. I went to the hospital thinking it was nothing serious. The doctor came in and said, "Well, we're not sure what's wrong. You're running on half a tank, and we are going to give you some blood." They gave me two units of blood that night. I tried to pin the doctor down as to what was wrong. He said, "I'm not sure. We're running some more tests. I'll tell you something on Saturday."

I'll never forget Dr. Upshaw. He was always whistling—just walking down the hall every day was a great experience for him. He walked into my room whistling, sat down, and said, "Danny, I have some good news and some bad news. Which do you want to hear first?" I said, "Well, Doc, go on and give it to me." He said, "Well, the bad news is you have AML, acute myeloblastic leukemia. The good news is I believe we can cure it. Ten years ago I would have told you that you had a year to live, but with the technology available today, we really feel that we can cure you." He did use the word "cure." He wanted to do a bone marrow test and a blood workup on all my siblings (I have six brothers and one sister). He also told me that he was going to start me on chemo on Monday. All the time, in my mind, I was saying, "Doc, you little short fellow, you don't know what you're talking about. I'm not *that* sick." I rejected my illness; this just couldn't be happening to me.

As I went through treatment, I had some sick days, though Dr. Upshaw told me that I was the only person he had ever known who gained weight while on chemotherapy. I was in the Baptist East Memorial Hospital in Memphis, Tennessee, for thirty days during this first treatment. Although I knew the Lord was in control, I kept thinking, "Why me? Why are all these things happening to me? I am a minister, and my faith is quivering. This isn't supposed to happen."

After thirty days in the hospital, I was in remission, and they allowed me to go home on New Year's Eve. I managed to make it home to be part of a New Year's party with my church family. I really enjoyed that time with them.

I kept thinking "Why me? Why are all these things happening to me?"

Although I had lost part of my hair—I didn't lose it all with my first chemotherapy—I had picked up weight. I was weak, but within a week or so, I was back in full swing. I noticed that I was changing; the Lord began working in my life. I began to be a little more effective, a little more sensitive to those who were critically ill. Things that I once thought were so important had become less important, and things that I didn't think were as important had become more important.

I continued going to the doctors, and Dr. Upshaw was so good. He said, "Danny, we need to harvest your bone marrow now. It's in really good shape, and if your leukemia ever comes back, we can give your own bone marrow to you." He continued, "We don't want to freeze bad bone marrow. Let's set up another bone marrow test just to make sure it's okay, and then two days later we will harvest it." When the test results came back, Dr. Upshaw said, "Danny, I have some bad news for you. Your leukemia is already back. I still say we can lick this thing, but we need to send you to Washington University Medical

Center in St. Louis to see Dr. Brown. We need to do a bone marrow transplant, and Dr. Brown is an expert in this field. We've done the blood work and tests on all your siblings; your sister is a perfect match. This will be difficult, but we believe it will work. We want Dr. Brown to interview and test you to make sure that you are a suitable candidate for a transplant." (At the time, I was thirty-nine years old and bone marrow transplants weren't done after the age of forty.)

I will never forget the ride home after learning the results of this bone marrow test. Evelyn, my wife, was almost in despair. I was kind of sulking and asking again, "Why me, Lord?" When we got home, we prayed and tried to decide how we were going to tell the congregation. Everyone was up because I had been in remission. The congregation knew that I had gone for a bone marrow test; we had to tell them the results. After hearing the results, the congregation became even more supportive of us.

Things moved rather fast. In January, we went to St. Louis and began the tests. The results came back, and Dr. Brown said, "Danny, you have two options. One option is to have the bone marrow transplant. If you do that, you will be in the hospital anywhere from ninety to a hundred days. Right now we have a 90 percent success rate with this treatment. Ten percent die from the treatment alone." Of course, that scared us.

The other option was to receive a severe round of radiation and chemotherapy and go home. The success rate of that was about 60 percent . Each time I went into remission and the cancer returned, my chance for healing would decrease.

Dr. Brown didn't want us to make a decision that day. Evelyn and I went back home. The doctor wanted me to call in my family, so Mom and Dad and my brothers and sister came. Of course, I had to ask my sister, Pamela, if she were willing to give me her bone marrow. She didn't hesitate for one moment. She said, "Danny, you didn't even have to ask. I am willing and ready now." I will never forget my sister and what she did for me. She was so loving, kind, responsive to my needs, and self-sacrificing. My family and the congregation were overwhelmingly support-ive of my decision to have the bone marrow transplant.

I had to ask my sister if she were willing to give me her bone marrow.

On February 28, 1991, we returned to Barnes Hospital at Washington University Medical Center in St. Louis, not know-ing what the end result would be but truly feeling that I was in the hands of God. Oh, I had all the questions, doubts, and fears that any person who is experiencing such a storm would have. I knew that I would have chemotherapy again. Since I had already been through it once, I decided I was going to be tough and take the chemotherapy sitting up. But there was a little more punch in this chemotherapy, and I got sick and had to lie down. So much for being tough. For the next six days, twenty-four hours a day, the poison went through my veins, killing the cancer that was in my blood. During the same time period, I also had five complete treatments of body radiation. I lost all the hair on my body, and, this time, I lost weight. My white blood cell count went down to nothing, and I became vulnerable to any type of virus or bacteria.

March 10 was D-day, the day I will never forget. That was the day when the leukemia cells in my body were at zero, totally wiped out, the day they gave me my sister's bone marrow. I knew this was the chance for me to either heal physically or to go and be with the Lord. At the end of the day I was really sick.

This was the chance to either heal physically or to go and be with the Lord.

On March 11, the doctors began watching for the white cell counts and all the blood counts to start increasing. For awhile there were none. That was scary! Then we got a few; then they jumped. During that time I began to evaluate my life and realized, "Hey, I'm thirty-nine years old, and I haven't accomplished the things I really want to accomplish for the Lord." I prayed, "Lord, you know, I have these children. I want to see my daughter, Stacey, graduate from high school. Lord, I really want to see her get married, and I would like to see some grandchildren. I want to see my son Daniel play baseball. I want to see him mature; I want to see him grow up and go to college." I thought about my younger son, Mark. And I feared for dear Evelyn. I worried about what would happen to her and how she would adjust. I thought about the pain she would experience when she saw me lying in the coffin on the day of my funeral.

My mother and Evelyn checked the charts every morning when they came in. Each day as the counts would go from 200 to 300, then later, from 3500 to 6000, I could see the excitement come into their faces. Then I became very, very sick. On days three, six, and nine, they used what they called a mop-up drug to make sure there were no more leukemia cells anywhere in my body. This drug made me unable to eat for about thirty days. During this time, I often thought just how long one hundred days in the hospital can be.

During this critical period of time, a special friend came to see me. Jerry had gone through some very difficult times in his life, and he told me that after his storm, he had gone into the "desert" for about a year. I could see that he had been put to the test and had come out on the other side stronger. I had been reading Philippians and was having trouble understanding how Paul could say, "For me, to live is Christ and to die is gain" (Phil. 1:21). How in the world could it be to Paul's gain to die? I was struggling—and still am struggling—to deal with death and dying. As Jerry was leaving that day, he said, "Danny, remember this: whatever happens will be good." I said, "Yes, that's right, Jerry." After he left, I began thinking about Paul's statement. I continued thinking about it after Evelyn went back to her room that night. I read Philippians 1 over and over again. I said to myself, "You know, Jerry is right. Whatever happens is good. If God decides to take me home to be with him, it will be good. If he spares my life and I stay here and try to make a difference and accomplish some things for the kingdom, it will be good." From that point on, my faith was rejuvenated.

Of course, visits from other Christians in the St. Louis area were helpful. And I remember Murial Pulliam, a blind lady whose ministry is to visit on the telephone with those who are in the hospital. I will never forget her voice. She was a great source of encouragement and strength.

As my health began to improve, I started to more deeply understand my relationship with God. I began to see the powerful effect that God was having in my life. I moved from the point of saying "God, this is just not fair! Why me?" to seeing how good God is. It dawned on me that life isn't fair, and that we probably have a lot of incorrect views on life—for instance, the idea that Christians don't have bad days. I learned that it doesn't matter—it really doesn't matter—whether you are having a great day or a rotten day. Every day, no matter what kind of day it is, is a great day in the Lord, because no matter what happens, God is in control and is so incredibly good. I am a beneficiary of the greatest heritage in the world—I am a son of God because of the supreme sacrifice of Jesus Christ. When the time for my earthly departure comes, it won't be a day of hopelessness or helplessness. Rather, it will be a day of victory, a day of celebrating true hope, true salvation, and true joy. It will be gain, not loss! It is joy to know that my loving, beautiful wife and my three dear children will also share in this inheritance.

I was dismissed from the hospital within six weeks, which was unheard of. I had to go back to St. Louis every two weeks, then once a month, then once every three months, then once every six months, then once a year, and eventually they turned me back over to Dr. Upshaw in Memphis, who finally released me from his care.

I watched Evelyn become more independent. She began taking care of our finances. The good church at Thyatira kept my paycheck coming and paid my bills during the whole time I was in the hospital. So many prayed for us. Some set up a fund to help with our expenses. I learned just how good Christians are, how good God is.

I thank God every day for what he has done for me, for how he has helped me to grow and become stronger. I have grown to the point that I understand that bad things do happen to good, Christian people. How powerful! How wonderful! How gracious! How good God really is!

When the time for my earthly departure comes, it won't be a day of hopelessness or helplessness.

I would like to share some of the lessons that I learned from this storm in my life. *I have learned that I can make a difference.* I am making a difference. I ran for the Mississippi State Senate because of my stand for Christian principles and values, to be a voice for Christian folks, and to show that government doesn't have to be corrupt. I speak at various youth rallies. The impact that death has on young people never ceases to amaze me. They sit in rapt attention and listen while I discuss passages of Scripture that exhort them to be more like Christ and to live for God. It's amazing.

I learned how important a positive attitude is. The doctors estimate that 90 percent of my successful cure can be attributed to my positive attitude. I could maintain a positive attitude, even when my faith wavered, because I knew who I belonged to and that whatever happened would be victory.

I have learned to be more sensitive to others. I have developed greater insight. I can walk with people through some of the unknowns and give them hope that they can get through their illness. And it's all because of God and what he can do—has done—through me. God has taken my life and helped me to be more effective in every area. I am a better father, a better husband, a better minister, and a much better communicator. Evelyn and I have become more equal in our relationship. We are partners. She no longer depends on me for everything. Although we need each other, it's different. We share in every aspect of our life.

I have grown to the point that I understand that bad things do happen to good, Christian people.

I think that my children have grown both positively and negatively through this experience. Stacey has grown in her spirituality and dependence on God. Daniel was bitter for awhile. Mark doesn't want me out of his sight. Of course, he's just nine. He's protective of me and wants to be with me as much as possible.

The number of lives that God has touched through me is unbelievable. I get calls from all over the nation to counsel with individuals who are going through bone marrow transplants or who have just been diagnosed with cancer and are struggling with the decision of what to do. The things that I can do now—I say "I" lightly, because it's really God doing it—I would never have imagined doing a few years ago. Coming through the storm has tempered me like heat tempers steel to make it stronger.

Coming through the storm has tempered me like heat tempers steel to make it stronger.

We're now beyond the storm. Every day we have peace in knowing who we are and knowing that we are going to make it. It doesn't matter what kind of day you're having or how bad the storm is, you will get beyond the storm and will have victory as a faithful Christian. Every person who keeps his eyes on Jesus is victorious.

—Danny Jackson

STORY THREE

Gary's STRUGGLE

My wife, Nancy, and I were married for nineteen years, but for seventeen of those years, she was ill. Her illnesses didn't hit all at once; they came in stages. And she steadily went downhill. There wasn't one particular thing that you could put your finger on that was wrong with Nancy. It wasn't cancer or leukemia or anything like that. It was just a steady physical decline: migraine headaches, back surgeries, diabetes, strokes, gall bladder trouble, and arthritis.

When I first met Nancy, she was sixteen years old, and I was nineteen. I thought she was beautiful. Our first year of marriage was just great. Nancy had been reared in a strict home, and now her whole focus became pleasing me. I enjoyed that! She really wanted children, and our first son, Gary Wayne, was born on September 7, 1973, one month before our first anniversary.

After Gary Wayne's birth, Nancy began to have migraine headaches, but with medication, they were tolerable. Our life seemed pretty normal—we were happily married, and we were raising a child.

However, something was missing from our lives, but I didn't know what. A friend from work came by the house occasionally and bugged us about going to church with him. I was nice to him, but told him I just wasn't interested. Finally, one day, Nancy and I decided to visit the church. It was great! God must have started working on me, because soon it wasn't enough just to go there. The minister asked us if we would like to study the Bible with him, and we agreed. After hearing the Gospel message we both gave our lives to Christ.

About four or five months into Nancy's second pregnancy, she began passing out. We didn't know what was causing her to pass out, but she told me that when she was a child she had passed out occasionally. Her parents had taken her to the hospital for a battery of tests, but the doctors didn't come up with anything concrete. I was a bit worried by the incidents, but Nancy didn't seem too bothered; so I tried not to worry.

Nancy and I had a great life together. We taught the kindergarten kids in Sunday School, and we worked on the bus ministry together. She deeply loved children, and she really loved the Lord. We had a great time working together. But her health began to take a few bad turns.

One morning, as she was getting up from the kitchen table, she twisted her back and was unable to straighten up. She had ruptured a disc in her lower back. Nancy soon had her first back surgery. When she came home from the hospital, a lot of people from church came over and helped out. I was so thankful for their help, but I also felt a little bad that I needed the help. I know this was a pride issue—and I struggle with it still—but as I look back on those days, I can see that the Lord and the Holy Spirit were there to help me. I didn't understand much about the Holy Spirit at that time, but he still took care of us. God knew how much each of us could handle, and fortunately, we had no idea what was in store for us.

Nancy's migraines continued, and her blood pressure began to soar. The doctor put her in the hospital for observation. While there, Nancy had a stroke. I am an eternal optimist and always want to make things better and to be in control, but for the first time I began to realize that this was out of my control. When I heard about her stroke, I cried and cried. I didn't understand it. Nancy recovered her speech, which was great. The first time she called me from the hospital, I couldn't quite understand her, but she was so proud when her speech returned. She never did quite regain full use of one hand.

I felt terribly alone, terribly lost, and terribly frustrated because I couldn't fix things for Nancy.

I remember the feeling I had on the way home from the hospital. I felt terribly alone, terribly lost, and terribly frustrated because I couldn't fix things for Nancy. I didn't know if her health was going to get better or not. I wanted it to get better. I thought, "God, I know you don't answer all these questions, but why? Why?" I kept asking myself, "Why is this happening?" (I know now that there isn't necessarily a reason for everything that happens.) I even considered going to a faith healer; I would have done anything to make this hurt get better or go away. In spite of my questions, I trusted God. I was strong in my faith, even though I didn't have a deep understanding of the Scriptures.

We adjusted; life went on—and so did the migraines. It's amazing, but each time we gained a little normalcy in our life— going out and doing things together, playing with the kids—it would slip away. Each time Nancy encountered a new health problem, things would get a little worse. During this time the people at church were awesome. My faith in God grew and so did my involvement in his work. I was appointed a deacon. Nancy and I continued to be involved in the bus ministry and the jail ministry.

But Nancy's health continued to go downhill. Arthritis set in, and then her gall bladder had to be removed; she lost a lot of feeling on her left side, particularly in her leg and back. The migraines increased tremendously. Some days she had to be alone with absolutely no light. Once or twice she passed out at church.

I didn't know what to do. I knew I couldn't run away, but I wanted to so badly. I frequently reminded myself of God's promise in 1 Corinthians 10:13—that he wouldn't give me any more than I could handle. However, at times I felt that he really stretched it on a lot of things. I don't know if it was the Holy Spirit, his Word, other Christians, or a combination of all three, but Nancy and I were able to keep on going.

God kept Nancy really close to him. She loved to listen to sermon tapes. We attended a Bible seminar in St. Louis, once, when she was feeling well, and she truly enjoyed it.

I could see that she had so much to offer God in his service, and I would grow angry sometimes because I couldn't understand why God didn't heal her so she could serve him fully. But I couldn't give up. I couldn't just give up on God—he was my only hope.

I knew I couldn't run away, but I wanted to so badly.

Eventually, the insurance company refused to sell us any more insurance. Every time Nancy had to go to the hospital, I would have to sell something to pay the hospital bill.

Nancy had to endure two more back surgeries. I specifically remember the last one. The doctor told her he wasn't sure that she would be able to stand the operation, but she wasn't able to stand the pain of the disc pressing against the nerve either. I remember being in the waiting room when the doctor told me that she might not make it through the operation. There was a small dark corner of my mind that responded, "Lord, let this be a release for her." But what made me feel so bad was that I felt it would be a release for me. And I felt so ashamed for having had that thought. She got through that operation.

Nancy was a beautiful person. She endured so much: numerous hospital visits, arthritis, a stroke, passing out, severe migraines, diabetes, and rapid resting-heart-rate. She endured the nurses' frustration as they tried to find one of her tiny veins to start IVs and the resulting black and blue bruises on her arms.

But she never complained, and her belief in God never wavered. Her faith is what helped me through a lot of it.

But seventeen years is a long time. Sometimes Nancy worried because she felt unable to fulfill her responsibilities as a mother. Our vacations consisted of visits to a doctor in Chicago. We would get a nice hotel just outside of Chicago, and we would make it the best we could for the boys. Nancy would watch the kids play from the room. She truly loved them. I have received several compliments about my children, but Nancy was the one who taught them.

Seventeen years is a long time when your wife is unable to be a wife to you. I did a lot of things alone, but I didn't want to be alone. I went shopping, to the movies, and to church alone. During this whole time God would send speakers, Bible lessons, and specific Scriptures my way that would carry me through. But still my heart ached and my soul groaned. I remember feeling at times that everyone had someone but me. I thought to myself, "I'm the only married single I know." That hurt. I wanted a mate to hold and to hold me back, and I didn't have that.

It was during one of those times, when I was feeling especially lonely, that I finally gave it all to God. I was sitting in the church parking lot watching couples come out holding hands, hugging each other, or going out to dinner together. It hurt so badly that I thought I couldn't stand it. I remember thinking, "Okay, God. I give up. I'm not going to fight anymore. I don't know what you want. I don't know if Nancy is going to get better, but I give up. I'm here; I'm not going anywhere. I give it all to you. It's yours. I'm here, if this is the way it has to be until I die, that's okay, God, because you are there." Once I fully gave it to him and let him take control, he was able to do something with me. I wasn't sure what God had in store for us, but I knew that he was the only answer. He was my only hope, Nancy's only hope, our only hope. I couldn't give up hope.

Our congregation started a support group for people with addictions and their familes approximately a year before Nancy passed away. The support, fellowship, and encouragement that I received at church kept me going. The support group didn't press me to talk. I could go and just sit, or I could talk about any-thing—it didn't matter. What I said didn't have to make sense; it didn't have to be scripturally right; it didn't have to fall in order. I could just be me. Because of my pride, I hated to cry, but once I started, I thought I was never going to stop. It was as if a dam had broken. Even now, reliving it through this writing brings up a lot of emotions. But I know that as long as I have the Lord and the church family I will be okay.

I was at a support group meeting when the last call came about my wife. The kids had come home and found Nancy where she had fallen in the bedroom. I was coming out of the meeting when Jim Watters walked up to me and said, "You need to go home right away. They need you there." He didn't say exactly what had happened. I remember driving home from church onto to our dead-end street and seeing the ambulance as it left for the hospital. I remember feeling a sense of panic and thinking, "God, not this way. Not this way." But it was his way and not my way. I remember the hospital; I remember going in to see her lifeless body in the emergency room; I remember the funeral home. Through it all, God taught me that I could do everything through him.

Nancy passed away on August 12, 1991. She was an awesome woman. I know she is in heaven, and I know God is caring for her. She gave me two great sons, and she did everything in her power to be the wife she wanted to be. I look back on some of my thoughts, and I am disgusted with myself. There were times when I wished she would go ahead and die. That's a sickening thought, and I don't like sharing it with people because I don't want them to think that I am some kind of terrible human. As I look back I realize that, until I was ready to give up control of my wife's life, my life, and my own destiny, I never found the peace I was looking for or truly allowed God to work in my life. The lesson that the Lord taught me—and is still teaching me—is that he is the one who controls the peace that I crave.

The lesson that the Lord taught me— and is still teaching me—is that he is the one who controls the peace that I crave.

The boys and I adjusted after Nancy's death. About three or four months after she died, I entered into a relationship that would have been disastrous had I pursued it. God saved me from that, and he later put someone else in my life. I have been married to Mary for two years now. She is the most fantastic person there ever was! I still care for my first wife, but I love Mary very much. Mary and I had been friends for a long time; she knew my wife and my situation. She is a beautiful, loyal person, inside and out.

Here is my lesson, relearned again: God is there, willing to help and provide for you. He wants to do it. He wants to love me and take care of me, but I have to be willing to let him, to let the Holy Spirit lead.

The hope and joy that I now have are awesome. I know that no matter what, God will to take care of me and my family and give me the strength I need.

—Gary Pierce

PART TWO

Assurance

Assurances from

God's Word

CHAPTER 5

Assurances from **God's Word**

Is God Really With Me?

The storms of life have a way of unsettling everything we thought was certain. Family members who were once taken for granted may be suddenly gone. Financial security can be wiped out in a few short months, or weeks, or even days. Comfortable roles and the security of relationships can be turned upside down in an instant.

When the wind blows and the lightening flashes and our world falls apart, the "big" questions of life and death and purpose and eternity force their way into our minds, and our souls cry out for answers. We need assurances—solid assurances—that we are not alone, that we are not forgotten. Most of all, we want to know that *God* has not forgotten us—that he has not left us alone.

"I will be with you."

God understands our need to know that *he is with us* and has assured us of his presence again and again throughout his Word. One of the key phrases used throughout the Bible is, *"I will be with you."* To Isaac he said, "Stay in this land for a while, and *I will be with you* and will bless you" (Gen. 26:3); to Jacob, "Go back to the land of your fathers . . . and *I will be with you*" (Gen. 31:3); and to Joshua, "No one will be able to stand up against you all the days of your life. As I was with Moses, *so I will be with you;* I will never leave you nor forsake you" (Josh. 1:5).

The same promise is repeated in the books of Isaiah, Jeremiah, and Haggai. (Isa. 41:10; Jer. 1:8, 19; 15:20; 30:11; 42:11; 46:28; Hag. 1:13; 2:4) Do you get the idea that God wants to assure us of his presence? No matter how loud the roar of the storm becomes, no matter the strength of the wind or the force of the rain, *God is with us!* He has not left us alone.

The story of Joseph is one of the most beautiful Old Testament testimonies of God's presence in the lives of humans. It shines as a beacon of promise of God's neverfailing presence. When Joseph's brothers abandoned him and sold him into slavery, God never left his side. God stayed with him and blessed all he did. Even the Egyptian Potiphar recognized that Joseph's success was the Lord's doing.

> *The Lord was with Joseph* and he prospered, and he lived in the house of his Egyptian master. When his master saw that the Lord was with him and that the Lord gave him success in everything he did, Joseph found favor in his eyes and became his attendant. (Gen. 39:2–5)

No matter how loud the roar of the storm becomes, no matter the strength of the wind or the force of the rain, *God is with us!*

When Joseph was thrown into prison after Potiphar's wife falsely accused him (Gen. 39:9–10), God continued to be with him and grant him success.

> While Joseph was there in the prison, *the Lord was with him;* he showed him kindness and granted him favor in the eyes of the prison warden. . . . The warden paid no attention to anything under Joseph's care, because *the Lord was with Joseph* and gave him success in whatever he did. (Gen. 39:20–23)

King David is also a source of great encouragement to us. Even one of Saul's servants recognized God's constant presence with David and described him thus:

He is a brave man and a warrior. He speaks well and is a fine-looking man. *And the Lord is with him.* (1 Sam. 16:18)

David was a successful commander because the Lord was with him. His ability to triumph over all the enemies of Israel was well known:

In everything he did he had great success, *because the Lord was with him.* (1 Sam. 18:14)

Why do you think these stories are recorded for us? "For everything that was written in the past was written to teach us, so that through endurance and the encouragement of the Scriptures we might have hope" (Rom. 15:4).

The stories of Old Testament heroes are recorded for our benefit. God recorded them so that you would have hope as you endure the storms in your life.

Adversity doesn't mean that God has abandoned you.

The same powerful God who helped Joseph overcome the treachery of his brothers and who helped David kill the feared Philistine warrior (1 Sam. 17:45–47) is available to you and me. The stories of Joseph and David are like lighthouses on a dark night, giving hope and consolation to those who face difficult and discouraging situations.

Joseph's and David's successes reassure us today that we, too, can triumph over great odds. Adversity doesn't mean that God has abandoned you; his promise to see you through will carry you to the next day . . . and the next day . . . and the next—one day at a time.

My favorite song of faith is "He Leadeth Me." In May 1983, I was in my office when I learned that I might be terminated from my job of seventeen years. I hung up the phone, met Claudette, and went to my oldest daughter's high school graduation. As I sat down, I told Claudette about the phone call and what I had just learned. The graduation ceremony began with the song "He Leadeth Me." I was unable to sing, so I sat, listened, and wept.

> He leadeth me: O blessed thought!
>> O words with heav'nly comfort fraught!
> Whate'er I do, where're I be,
>> Still 'tis God's hand that leadeth me.
>
> Sometimes 'mid scenes of deepest gloom,
>> Sometimes where Eden's bowers bloom,
> By waters still, o'er troubled sea,
>> Still 'tis God's hand that leadeth me.
>
> Lord, I would clasp Thy hand in mine,
>> Nor ever murmur nor repine;
> Content, whatever lot I see,
>> Still 'tis God's hand that leadeth me.
>
> And when my task on earth is done,
>> When by Thy grace the vict'ry's won,
> E'en death's cold wave, I will not flee,
>> Since God thro' Jordan leadeth me.

He leadeth me, He leadeth me,
By His own hand, He leadeth me;
His faithful follow'r I would be,
For by His hand He leadeth me.

The storm clouds that had gathered over my head that day brought new meaning to those old, familiar words. I stand today as living proof of God's faithfulness to his promise to be with those who put their faith and trust in him and who refuse to do wrong. I thank God for the turn my journey of life took that day when God showed me what he meant when he said *I will be with you.*

There's no need to fear.

The fact that the Bible tells us not to be afraid so many times indicates that God understands that we *are* afraid. God's frequent statements telling us not to fear are not harsh rebukes, but comforting assurances that there's *no need to fear,* because he is with us.

God's frequent statements telling us not to fear are not harsh rebukes, but comforting assurances that there's no need to fear.

Over and over in the Bible, God's admonitions not to fear offer calming assurances. As you read the following words, spoken by a loving God to his beloved creation, hear them as spoken to yourself, for God offers the same message to you in your painful storm.

Abraham was the first Old Testament hero whose fears were calmed by God.

> The Lord came to Abram in a vision: *"Do not be afraid, Abram. I am your shield, your very great reward."* (Gen. 15:1)

God told Isaac, *"Do not be afraid, for I am with you"* (Gen. 26:24), and he reassured Jacob,

> *Do not be afraid* to go down to Egypt, for I will make you into a great nation there. I will go down to Egypt with you. (Gen. 46:3–4)

Through Moses, God assured the Israelites:

> The Lord himself goes before you and will be with you; he will never leave you nor forsake you. *Do not be afraid;* do not be discouraged. (Deut. 31:8)

In the book of Isaiah, God assures the Israelites by reminding them of the past.

> I took you from the ends of the earth,
>   from its farthest corners I called you.
> I said, "You are my servant";
>   I have chosen you and have not rejected you.
> So *do not fear,* for I am with you;
>   *do not be dismayed,* for I am your God.

I will strengthen you and help you;
I will uphold you with my righteous right hand.
(Isa. 41:9–10)

God told his children that since he had cared for them in the past, they shouldn't be afraid of the future because he would continue to be with them. We, too, have the same assurance. Look back at your life. Remember the times God has strengthened you and brought you through other storms. Because of what he has done in the past, you can be assured that he will be with you today.

In a second passage from Isaiah, God goes even further in his promise to be with his children.

Fear not, for I have redeemed you;
I have summoned you by name; you are mine.
When you pass through the waters,
I will be with you;
and when you pass through the rivers,
they will not sweep over you.
When you walk through the fire,
you will not be burned;
the flames will not set you ablaze. . . .
Since you are precious and honored in my sight,
and because I love you,
I will give men in exchange for you,
and people in exchange for your life.
Do not be afraid, for I am with you.
(Isa. 43:1–5)

Are you passing through high waters? Do strong currents threaten to sweep over you? Are you walking through the fire of pain. These words of comfort are for you.

History has shown that God was faithful in his promises to save the Israelites. Israel suffered under the force of many oppressing world powers, but in the end God delivered them. God never forsakes his people!

"When you pass through the rivers, they will not sweep over you. When you walk through the fire, you will not be burned."

Assurances to calm our fears are not confined to the Old Testament. Beginning with the birth of Christ, we hear the sweet words over and over, *"Do not be afraid."* As you read through the following Scriptures, notice how many times the person being comforted is called by *name*. God knows your name, and he says to you, "Do not be afraid, _____, for I am with you." When the angel appeared to Zechariah to announce the birth of John the Baptist, he said, *"Do not be afraid,* Zechariah; your prayer has been heard" (Luke 1:13); to Mary, the mother of Jesus, the angel said, *"Do not be afraid,* Mary, you have found favor with God" (Luke 1:30); and to the shepherds in the hills who heard the news of the coming Savior, the angel said, *"Do not be afraid.* I bring you good news of great joy that will be for all the people" (Luke 2:10).

Jesus, speaking to his disciples, said,

> *Do not be afraid,* little flock, for your Father has been pleased to give you the kingdom. (Luke 12:32)

See how tenderly Jesus speaks to his disciples. He calls them "little flock" and tells them that the Father is "pleased" to give them the kingdom. His tender words are for you too.

In John 14, as Jesus prepares his disciples for his departure, he says,

> Peace I leave with you; my peace I give you. . . . Do not let your hearts be troubled and *do not be afraid.* (John 14:27)

The apostle Paul also recieved comfort from the Lord. When Paul faced the challenges of teaching the people of Corinth, he was afraid: "I came to you in weakness and *fear,* and with *much trembling"* (1 Cor. 2:3). In response to Paul's fears, God came to him in a vision and said,

> *Do not be afraid;* keep on speaking, do not be silent. For I am with you, and no one is going to attack and harm you. (Acts 18:9–10)

Because Paul was well acquainted with the Old Testament "I will be with you" and "Do not be afraid" passages, when God told him not to be afraid and assured him that he would be with him, Paul had a firm foundation for his confidence.

We, too, have this same foundation. Because we have so many historical accounts of God's faithful, never-failing care, we can boldly trust him to take care of us.

Besides calming us and filling our hearts with peace, God's assurances that we don't need to be afraid also instill us with *courage*—courage to stand firm when the storms come.

As the Israelites were readying to cross the Red Sea, they looked up and saw the massive Egyptian army barreling down on them, and the Bible says they were "terrified." Assurances of the Lord's commitment to see them through came through Moses:

> *Do not be afraid. Stand firm* and you will see the deliverance the Lord will bring you today. (Exod. 14:13)

The same God who fought the enemies of the Israelites will fight the enemies in your life. Your job is to place your trust in him, to take your stand beside him, and to allow him to bring about the victory.

God can be trusted.

Part of the pain of the storms of life is often the *loss of trust.* When hopes and dreams are dashed to the shore by the fierce winds of pain, how can we ever trust again? Can anyone be trusted? Can God be trusted?

The Bible assures us over and over again that God *can,* indeed, be trusted.

- God promised Eve that her offspring would one day crush the head of the serpent's offspring—and he did!

- God promised Abram that he would have a son in his old age—and he did!

- God promised Moses that water would come out of a rock—and it did!

- God promised the Israelites that he would bring them safely out of Egypt and into the Promise Land—and he did!

- God promised Gideon that he would fight the battle for him against the Midianites, using only trumpets, torches, and pitchers—and he did!
- God promised Hannah that he would give her a son—and he did!
- God promised the world that he would send a Savior—and he did!
- God promised us that he would raise Jesus from the dead—and he did!
- And God has promised you that he will work everything together for good for those who love him—and he will!

Our God is a God who can be trusted. He will never desert or betray you—even if people you love do.

Trusting God does not mean that things will always turn out as we desire.

But trusting God does not mean that things will always turn out as we desire. The Romans 8:28 passage is often misunderstood:

> We know that all things work together for good for those who love God, who are called according to his purpose. (NRSV)

This verse does not say that everything in our lives will be good, but that God will work everything *together* for good. God takes the bad that Satan throws our way, and he weaves it into the tapestry of our lives. And sometimes it takes *time* for us to see God's working in our lives. It isn't easy to wait on God while going through trials, but that is what trials require—endurance and patience. A plaque in my house reads, "God give me patience—and I want it right now!" My timetable is usually different from God's, but he won't abandon me if I have placed my trust in him.

The book of Daniel is a great faith-building book for those who want to learn how to trust God. When Shadrach, Meshach, and Abednego were taken captive by King Nebuchadnezzar of Babylon, along with many other Israelites, their trust was put to the test.

King Nebuchadnezzar set up a golden image and ordered all to worship it; these three young men refused. When Nebuchadnezzar learned of their refusal to bow, he gave them one last chance to submit. "But if you do not worship it, you will be thrown immediately into a blazing furnace. Then what god will be able to rescue you from my hand?" (Dan. 3:15).

Their answer stands as an example of trust for all ages:

> If we are thrown into the blazing furnace, the God we serve is able to save us from it, and he will rescue us from your hand, O king. But *even if he does not*, we want you to know, O king, that we will not serve your gods or worship the image of gold you have set up. (Dan. 3:17–18)

Shadrach, Meshach and Abednego appended their proclamation of faith by saying that even if God didn't deliver them, nothing would change! They laid it on the line and never faltered. What a response of faith! When put to the test, they acted out of conviction, not fear. Fear would have caused them to compromise and bow down to the image of gold, but conviction demanded a faithfulness that even the threat of death could not destroy. Trusting God means trusting him *no matter what.*

We, too, must make our decision to serve God no matter what—*before* the trial comes. If we wait until we are in the middle of a trial to decide where our allegiance lies, fear and discouragement can easily dampen our trust.

In 1992, two years before Claudette's death on November 10, 1994, she wrote an article for the *Christian Woman* magazine titled "My Last Birthday." She cited the example of these three Hebrew young men. She believed that God could heal her of cancer, but even if he didn't, she would not deny him. She showed the same faith as Shadrach, Meshach, and Abednego. What a wonderful modern example!

Not once has our God gone back on a promise, and he has promised that he will work all of your life together for good. Satan means you harm by sending pain, heartache, and fear into your life; but God will take Satan's evil and work it into your life for good. Our God is a God who can be trusted.

God will protect you.

When the whirling winds and pelting rain of the storm press upon us, we want relief and protection from the harshness of pain. We, like King David, cry out for God's protection:

I am in pain and distress; may your salvation, O God, protect me. (Ps. 69:29)

The book of Psalms is a wonderful refuge for weary storm-travelers seeking protection. Throughout the Psalms, we are sometimes surprised by David's honesty with God about his feelings, for he openly expressed his despair, his fears, and his pain. And in the Psalms we also see that whenever David expressed negative feelings about his situation—and even toward God—he always worked his way through his feelings and came to a proclamation of God's unfailing love and constant protection.

Be comforted by the expressions of God's protection in the following psalms. Notice the terms David used to describe God—*rock, fortress, refuge, hiding place,* and *shield.* God truly is our protector.

> He is a *shield*
> for all who take *refuge* in him.
> For who is God besides the Lord?
> And who is the *Rock* except our God?
> It is God who arms me with strength
> and makes my way perfect.
> He makes my feet like the feet of a deer;
> he enables me to stand on the heights.
> (Ps. 18:30–33)

> I sought the Lord, and he answered me;
> he delivered me from all my fears.
> Those who look to him are radiant;
> their faces are never covered with shame. . . .
> Taste and see that the Lord is good;
> blessed is the man who takes *refuge* in him. . . .

The lions may grow weak and hungry,
　　but those who seek the Lord lack no good thing. . . .
The righteous cry out, and the Lord hears them;
　　he delivers them from all their troubles.
The Lord is close to the brokenhearted
　　and saves those who are crushed in spirit.
A righteous man may have many troubles,
　　but the Lord delivers him from them all;
he protects all his bones,
　　not one of them will be broken.
　　　　　　　　　　　　(Ps. 34:4–5, 8, 10, 17–20)

Find rest, O my soul, in God alone;
　　my hope comes from him.
He alone is my *rock* and my salvation;
　　he is my *fortress,* I will not be shaken.
My salvation and my honor depend on God;
　　he is my mighty *rock,* my *refuge.*
Trust in him at all times, O people;
　　pour out your hearts to him,
　　for God is our *refuge.* . . .
One thing God has spoken,
　　two things have I heard:
that you, O God, are strong,
　　and that you, O Lord, are loving.
　　　　　　　　　　　　(Ps. 62:5–8, 11–12)

You are *my hiding place;*
　　you will *protect* me from trouble
　　and surround me with songs of deliverance.
　　　　　　　　　　　　(Ps. 32:7)

Satan wants to hurt us. His desire is that the storms of life destroy us and separate us from the love of our heavenly Father. But Jesus prayed for us that this would not happen—what a wonderful thought to think that Jesus has prayed for our protection.

> I will remain in the world no longer, but they are still in the world, and I am coming to you. Holy Father, *protect* them by the power of your name—the name you gave me—so that they may be one as we are one. (John 17:11)

> My prayer is not that you take them out of the world but that you *protect* them from the evil one. (John 17:15)

"The Lord is close to the brokenhearted and saves those who are crushed in spirit."

And finally, hear this assurance from the apostle Paul, who knew the meaning of trials, who knew the storms of life:

> The Lord is faithful, and he will strengthen and *protect* you from the evil one. (2 Thess. 3:3)

Storms will come into our lives; but they will not sweep us away, for God is with us. Hear these words of Paul and be assured that the same God who was with him is with you also.

> We are hard pressed on every side, but not crushed; per-
> plexed, but not in despair; persecuted, but not aban-
> doned; struck down, but not destroyed. (2 Cor. 4:8–9)

Victory is assured.

Wouldn't it be great to know that victory was assured before
you entered a battle? Even though you knew the battle would be
hard and even though you knew you would suffer damage,
wouldn't it be great to know—without a doubt—that victory
was yours?

You *can* know this! Our God is a God of victory, and he
assures victory for his children.

> When you go to war against your enemies and see
> horses and chariots and an army greater than yours. . . .
> do not be fainthearted or afraid; do not be terrified or
> give way to panic before them. For the Lord your God
> is the one who goes with you to fight for you against
> your enemies to give you victory. (Deut. 20: 1, 3–5)

Do you hear that! When the enemies in your life—loneliness,
fear, uncertainty, doubt—when these enemies come upon you
and their army seems greater than yours, you do not need to
"give way to panic" because the Lord is the one who fights for
you!

One of the greatest Old Testament stories illustrating God's
commitment to lead us to victory is found in 2 Chronicles 20.

When the Moabites and Ammonites made war on Jehoshaphat, king of Judah, the Israelites were vastly outnumbered and outpowered. From a human or military standpoint, an Israelite victory was impossible, but the battle became a demonstration of God's faithfulness and power.

In a passionate plea to God for help, Jehoshaphat said,

> If calamity comes upon us, whether the sword of judgment, or plague or famine, we will stand in your presence before this temple that bears your Name and will cry out to you in our distress, and you will hear us and save us. . . . We have no power to face this vast army that is attacking us. We do not know what to do, but *our eyes are upon you.* (2 Chron. 20:8–9, 12)

What a statement of absolute helplessness and absolute trust!

The Lord sent a message to Jehoshaphat through Jahaziel, "Do not be afraid or discouraged because of this vast army. For the battle is not yours, but God's" (2 Chron. 20:15). Can you imagine the people's reaction when they heard the announcement: *"The battle is not yours, but God's"?* What an empowering message!

Jahaziel told the men of Judah to simply go down to meet the army.

> You will not have to fight this battle. Take up your positions; stand firm and see the deliverance the Lord will give you. . . . Go out to face them tomorrow, and the Lord will be with you. (2 Chron. 20:17)

The people of Judah didn't know what the outcome would be, but their faith carried them forward. They gathered strength from God's promise. And God delivered them!

We, too, have enemies to fight—enemies like fear and loneliness and frustration and discouragement—and our only hope is to put our eyes on God! God says to us what he said to Judah: "You will not have to fight this battle. Take up your positions; stand firm and see the deliverance the Lord will give you. . . . Go out to face [your enemy], and the Lord will be with you."

The situation may look impossible, and defeat may appear inevitable. However, we must believe that the same God who remained faithful and loyal to his people in the Old Testament will rescue us. God has proven himself to be faithful over and over again. Why should we think any less of God today than did those who lived hundreds of years ago?

Judah demonstrated their faith in God by taking their position and standing firm. It was up to them to take their position, and it was up to God to deliver. Likewise, we must take a stand before God will deliver!

The people of Judah didn't know what the outcome would be, but their faith carried them forward. They gathered strength from God's faithful adherence to his past promises of "I will be with you." Your strength, too, lies in this promise.

CHAPTER 6

Assurances from **God's Word**

Does God Really Care?

When we cry for help and beg for relief and it doesn't come, we begin to wonder if God is aware of our needs. When the pain escalates to an almost unbearable level and comfort is an unrealistic dream, we may whisper words of doubt: "Does God really care? Does he know what I'm feeling? Is he able to respond? Where are his promised comforts?"

The painful periods of waiting are breeding grounds for doubts and fear. We need solid assurances from God's Word that will give us the courage to hold on, that will provide firm footing beneath our sinking feet.

And the joyous news is that God *does* care, that he *knows* our needs, and that he *will* respond with real help and loving comfort.

God loves unconditionally.

When the storms of life plow through us, our sense of worth is often torn to shreds and we may wonder if anyone can love us just as we are—unconditionally.

For the men and women whose stories you read in the first section of this book, the source of unconditional, totally dependable love was always their heavenly Father.

A most touching demonstration of this love is seen in the book of Hosea. The Israelites had broken God's heart by their rebellious ways. They had given their affections to other gods and their lives were filled with wickedness. The agony of God's heart is revealed in this mournful lament: "I long to redeem them but they speak lies against me. . . . I trained them and strengthened them, but they plot evil against me" (Hos. 7:13, 15). God had blessed them and cared for them, yet they turned from him.

But we see the extent of his love—a love that *could not, would not* let them go—in these powerful words:

> How can I give you up, Ephraim?
>   How can I hand you over, Israel? . . .
> My heart is changed within me;
>   all my compassion is aroused.

I will not carry out my fierce anger. . . .
For I am God, and not man.

(Hos. 11:8–9)

If God loved these rebellious, ungrateful children through all of their affairs with false gods and their craving after what the other nations had, surely he will and does love us—unconditionally.

A look at the life of Christ also reveals the amazing, unconditional love of our Father. The weeping woman in Luke 7, who washed the feet of Jesus with her tears and dried them with her hair, experienced the unconditional love of God. An uninvited guest, this woman dared to enter a room full of judgmental men just to be close to Jesus. When Simon, the host, saw what this woman was doing, he thought to himself, "If this man were a prophet, he would know who is touching him and what kind of woman she is—*that she is a sinner*" (Luke 7:39). Jesus' response was to rebuke Simon with a story about debts and forgiveness. He stood up for the condemned woman and, in front of all those judgmental leaders, he loved her unconditionally.

The classic story of God's unconditional love is the story of the Prodigal Son. The story is about a thoughtless, rebellious son, who demanded his inheritance—while his father was still living—and took it to a far country and wasted it on wild living. When this reckless boy had spent all his money, he found himself serving slop to pigs in a pigpen. And when his heart was finally broken and he decided to return home to his father, we see this loving father *waiting* for his son at the end of the road.

> While [the boy] was still a long way off, his father saw him and was filled with compassion for him; he ran to his son, threw his arms around him and kissed him. The

> son said to him, "Father, I have sinned against heaven and against you. I am no longer worthy to be called your son." But the father said to his servants, "Quick! Bring the best robe and put it on him. Put a ring on his finger and sandals on his feet. Bring the fattened calf and kill it. Let's have a feast and celebrate. For this son of mine was dead and is alive again; he was lost and is found." (Luke 15:20–24)

This father's love was unconditional—the kind of love we all long for. And this is the love our heavenly Father has for us.

In Jesus' Sermon on the Mount, Jesus revealed God's unconditional love for us in his teachings on how we are to love others.

> Love your enemies and pray for those who persecute you, that you may be sons of your Father in heaven. He causes his sun to rise on the evil and the good, and sends rain on the righteous and the unrighteous. (Matt. 5:44–45)

God's love is not based on *who we are,* but on *who he is.* God's very nature is love.

> And so we know and *rely on* the love God has for us. *God is love.* (1 John 4:16)

God *is* love, and he loves us with a love that can be relied on.

One of the most assuring passages on the unconditional nature of God's love tells us in strong words of affirmation that if God loved us while we were his enemies, we can certainly count on him to love us now that we are his children. Take the time to read these powerful words:

> You see, at just the right time, when we were still powerless, Christ died for the ungodly. Very rarely will any-

one die for a righteous man, though for a good man someone might possibly dare to die. But God demonstrates his own love for us in this: While we were still sinners, Christ died for us. Since we have now been justified by his blood, how much more shall we be saved from God's wrath through him! For if, when we were God's enemies, we were reconciled to him through the death of his Son, how much more, having been reconciled, shall we be saved through his life! (Rom. 5:6–10)

When circumstances make you want to cry out, "God, do you still love me?"—the resounding answer from our heavenly Father is *Yes!*

Love isn't just one of God's traits—it's who he is! How reassuring it is to know that you don't have to do anything to deserve God's love; all you need do is accept it. Knowing that you are loved by the creator of the universe should give you reassurance to face any storm.

God knows our needs.

Your Father knows what you need before you ask him. (Matt. 6:8)

Let's say it again.

Your Father knows what you need before you ask him.

Storms leave us weary and fearful. When the storm is past, we find that we've used every ounce of energy just to survive and we are often afraid of what will come next. We feel incapable and unable to meet the challenges ahead.

"For you created my inmost being; you knit me together in my mother's womb."

Your Father knows what you need before you ask him. He made you. He knows every part of you.

> O Lord, you have searched me and you know me.
> You know when I sit and when I rise;
>   you perceive my thoughts from afar.
> You discern my going out and my lying down;
>   you are familiar with all my ways.
> Before a word is on my tongue
>   you know it completely, O Lord. . . .
> For you created my inmost being;
>   you knit me together in my mother's womb.
> I praise you because I am fearfully and wonderfully made;
>   your works are wonderful,
>   I know that full well.
>   (Ps. 139:1–4, 13–14)

God's intimate knowledge of our needs combined with his unconditional love for each one of us adds up to comfort and assurance and peace for worn-out storm victims. If the Bible taught only that God *knows* us but not that he *loves* us, we would have no confidence. But, as his children, we are covered and protected by both his knowledge and his love.

Through the prophet Isaiah, our Father offers these soothing words of comfort and assurance:

> The Lord will guide you always;
>> he will satisfy your needs in a sun-scorched land
>> and will strengthen your frame.
> You will be like a well-watered garden,
>> like a spring whose waters never fail.
>> (Isa. 58:11)

Has your heart ever felt scorched by the heat of the storm? Has your "frame" ever felt shaken and weak? Wouldn't you love to feel refreshed like a "well-watered garden"? God knows your needs. He understands how you feel. He extends refreshment.

When he chooses not to calm the storm, he will calm you as the storm rages.

God doesn't promise to shield you from all the storms on the waters of life, but he will ease the crossing. When he chooses not to calm the storm, he will calm you as the storm rages. To know that God knows you and hears you, when perhaps no one else does, can make the storm bearable.

God will respond.

God loves us. He knows our needs. But will he respond? Will he provide relief when we cry out? The Bible assures us that he will.

> Ask and it will be given to you; seek and you will find; knock and the door will be opened to you. For everyone who asks receives; he who seeks finds; and to him who knocks, the door will be opened. (Matt. 7:7–8)

These verses offer absolute assurance that God will respond to our requests. Jesus explained *how* God responds with an example of how a Palestinian father would respond to his son. In Jesus' day, rocks were heated on an outside fire and then placed in an oven. When a person reached into the oven for a piece of bread, he could easily pick up a stone instead. However, a father wouldn't knowingly give a stone to his son when the son wanted bread. Jesus asked the question: "Which of you, if his son asks for bread, will give him a stone?" (Matt. 7:9). If an earthly father responds with love to his son's requests, will not our heavenly Father give us what we need? Jesus assures us that he will.

God's relief may not be immediate, but he will always come to the rescue. Our timetable for rescue may not be the same as God's, but we can be assured that he will respond.

Sometimes, however, we ask for things that aren't in our best interest, and then when God doesn't respond as we'd like, we think he's not responding at all. We should be grateful that *some* of our requests are not granted. Did you ever go to a high school reunion and see the boy or girl you almost married, but didn't? Do you remember praying diligently, in your high school days, that this person would love you, believing that this one was the one of your dreams? Do you remember how brokenhearted and disappointed you were when things didn't work out? And then when you saw your "loved one" at the twenty-year reunion, did you find yourself in the corner of the room thanking God for not answering that request? Sometimes God spares us from our own prayers.

God's relief may not be immediate, but he will always come to the rescue.

The well-known Sermon on the Mount offers sweet assurance of God's loving care through two beautiful illustrations from nature.

> Look at the birds of the air; they do not sow or reap or store away in barns, and yet your heavenly Father feeds them. Are you not much more valuable than they? . . .
> See how the lilies of the field grow. They do not labor or spin. Yet I tell you that not even Solomon in all his splendor was dressed like one of these. If that is how God clothes the grass of the field, which is here today and tomorrow is thrown into the fire, will he not much more clothe you, O you of little faith? (Matt. 6:26–30)

We are more valuable than birds and lilies. God takes care of them, and he promises to take care of us.

The psalmist David offers much insight into life's pain and God's response to it. David continually took his requests before God's throne, and his writings reveal that God faithfully answered him.

> To the Lord I cry aloud, and he *answers* me from his holy hill. (Ps. 3:4)

> I call on the Lord in my distress, and he *answers* me. (Ps. 120:1)

David's life was literally an open book. His pains, his struggles, his sins are laid wide open for all to see. Because David was so open in his communication with God, we can be encouraged to take our requests to him as well. We also see in David's life that God's answers did not always come in the form David wanted nor as quickly as David wanted. Twelve times in the book of psalms the psalmist asks the question, "How long?" (Pss. 6:3; 13:1–2; 35:17; 74:10; 79:5; 80:4; 82:2; 89:46; 90:13; 94:3; 119:84)

> *How long* must I wrestle with my thoughts and every day have sorrow in my heart? (Ps. 13:2)

> *How long,* O Lord? Will you hide yourself forever? (Ps. 89:46)

> *How long* must your servant wait? (Ps. 119:84)

David's despair is our despair. We cry out to the Lord, and we wait for an answer—and the answer doesn't seem to come. Yet, even as David expressed his despair, he always praised God and thanked him for his steadfast care. Hear the amazing conclusion of Psalm 13:

> But I trust in your unfailing love;
> my heart rejoices in your salvation.
> I will sing to the Lord, for he has been good to me.

What a heart! David was able to praise God and thank him because he trusted him absolutely—he trusted him to love him, to care for him, and to provide for him as he saw fit. This is the attitude God wants from us.

Nowhere has God promised to respond to our requests by granting our every desire or by making our lives easy. But he has promised to be with us in our pain and to provide for us what we truly need.

> And my God will meet all your needs according to his glorious riches in Christ Jesus. (Phil. 4:19)

As one author has stated, "It isn't the size of the bump that is the most important; it's the attitude of the bumpee as to whether he will become bitter or better."

God comforts lovingly.

When a storm has knocked us off our feet, blown us off course, and pounded us into the ground, we need assuring touches of hope—we need God's *comfort*. The book of 2 Corinthians describes God as the "Father of compassion," the

"God of all comfort." How comforting to know that our Father's nature is to be compassionate.

> Praise be to the God and Father of our Lord Jesus Christ, the *Father of compassion* and the *God of all comfort,* who comforts us in all our troubles, so that we can comfort those in any trouble with the comfort we ourselves have received from God. For just as the sufferings of Christ flow over into our lives, so also through Christ our comfort overflows. (2 Cor. 1:3–5)

When Jesus sees you weeping, he is deeply moved in his spirit and troubled, and he weeps with you.

Jesus revealed the compassion of the Father when he saw Mary weeping over the loss of her brother, Lazarus.

> When Jesus saw [Mary] weeping, and the Jews who had come along with her also weeping, he was deeply moved in spirit and troubled. . . . Jesus wept. (John 11:33, 35)

When Jesus sees you weeping, when he sees your pain, he is deeply moved in his spirit and troubled, and he weeps with you.

Understanding the heart of God allows us to know his comfort and be touched by his compassion. David knew God's heart and thus could say,

Even though I walk through the valley of the shadow of death, I will fear no evil, for you are with me; your rod and your staff, they comfort me. (Ps. 23:4)

Experienced storm-travelers know the sense of God's presence in their pain.

Can you identify with the words of this passage? Do you feel that you have walked or are walking through the "valley of the shadow of death"? Notice that David does not talk of being transported from this dark valley to one of peace and light, but he speaks of God's presence *with him* in the valley. Experienced storm-travelers—like the men and women in the first section of this book—who have cried to God for help, have come to know the sense of his presence in their pain. God's work in our lives does not mean exemption from pain, but it means that he walks *with* us in our valley of pain.

Does your pain ever drive you to a pit of despair? That's were Jeremiah the prophet ended up; and Jeremiah called to God from his pit. In lamenting the destruction of Jerusalem, Jeremiah expressed his pain and ours and offered assuring words of comfort:

> I called on your name, O Lord, from the *depths of the pit.* You heard my plea: "Do not close your ears to my cry for relief." You came near when I called you, and you said, "Do not fear." (Lam. 3:55–57)

God's amazing response to his cry was that he "came near." We are not alone in our pain. God is down there in the pit of pain with us.

Now read these additional words penned by the lamenting Jeremiah:

> Because of the Lord's great love we are not consumed, for his compassions never fail. They are new every morning; great is your faithfulness. (Lam. 3:22–23)

God's compassions never fail. The immediate pain of the storm is often unavoidable, but our God of compassion and comfort is ever near.

As children run to their mother for comfort, so we can find comfort in God:

> As a mother comforts her child, so will I comfort you. (Isa. 66:13)

God really does care.

CHAPTER 7

Assurances from **God's Word**

Is There Life Beyond This One?

When we talk about life after death, we're usually talking about *physical* death and life in *heaven*. But sometimes, the storms of this life leave the living feeling as though they were dead, as though their lives were over. For the Christian, the assurance of life after death lies in the empty tomb of Jesus Christ. His resurrection promises new life—both in this world and in the one to come.

Storms are only temporary.

Most of us are surprised by the storm, but the Bible tells us that storms are nothing out of the ordinary.

> Do not be surprised at the painful trial you are suffering, as though something strange were happening to you. (1 Pet. 4:12)

Peter, here, is talking about the trials that Christians were suffering because of the persecution, but the admonition speaks to us as well. The painful trials that we undergo are not "something strange"—they are the lot of humankind.

In spite of Peter's warning, we are usually surprised by the storm. It sneaks up on us and knocks us off our feet. Sometimes we even get angry with God, thinking that we don't deserve such pain, that, in essence, he owes us a storm-free life.

But nowhere in Scripture are we promised exemption from illness, sorrow, or death. We are, however, encouraged to look beyond this life to the next and there to find courage and joy. The apostle Paul, who suffered much in this life, penned these words:

> For our light and momentary troubles are achieving for us an eternal glory that *far outweighs* them all. So we fix our eyes *not on what is seen, but on what is unseen.* For what is seen is temporary, but what is unseen is eternal. (2 Cor. 4:17–18)

As real as your pain is, it is only temporary. Paul goes so far as to call it "light and momentary." When we're in the middle of the storm, our pain seems far from "light" and its duration anything but "momentary," but Paul reminds us that the eternal glory that awaits us "far outweighs" the troubles of this life—it's all a matter of comparison, he tells us.

Paul goes on to tell us how we can endure the pain. He tells us to "fix our eyes on what is unseen." Where we fix our eyes is a matter of *choice*. Paul tells us not to look at what is seen—for that is temporary—but to look at the unseen—the eternal. The voices from the storm in the first section of this book relay the message over and over that focusing on God, trusting in him, is the only way to survive the storm.

As real as your pain is, it is only temporary.

Sometimes the force of the storm is so powerful that we lose hope that things will get better. At times like these, we need to look beyond this life to the inheritance kept for us in heaven. Hear these words from Peter:

> [God] has given us new birth into a living hope *through the resurrection of Jesus Christ* from the dead, and into an inheritance that can never perish, spoil or fade—kept in heaven for you. . . . In this you greatly rejoice, though now for a little while you may have had to suffer grief in all kinds of trials. (1 Pet. 1:3–4, 6)

Because Jesus was raised—the previous Scripture says—because his tomb was empty, we have an inheritance in heaven that nothing can spoil. And this gives us reason to rejoice—even though we suffer grief for now. Heaven is ahead!

Life after death is assured.

For those in Christ, the assurances of life after death are abundant. The promise of the empty tomb is the ultimate hope of all humankind. Without such hope, this life is futile and meaningless. Jesus' words to Martha, the sister of Lazarus, are for us too.

> I am the resurrection and the life. He who believes in me *will live, even though he dies;* and whoever lives and believes in me will never die. (John 11:25–26)

The empty tomb is central to our whole system of faith. And because of our faith in the unseen, we see death as a passage into a new life:

> Listen, I tell you a mystery: We will not all sleep, but we will all be changed—in a flash, in the twinkling of an eye, at the last trumpet. For the trumpet will sound, the dead will be raised imperishable, and we will be changed. . . . When the perishable has been clothed with the imperishable, and the mortal with immortality, then the saying that is written will come true: "Death has been swallowed up in victory."

"Where, O death, is your victory?
Where, O death, is your sting?"
The sting of death is sin, and the power of sin is the law.
But thanks be to God! He gives us the victory through
our Lord Jesus Christ. (1 Cor. 15:51–57)

For those in the midst of grief, the words of the above Scripture may be difficult to understand. How can the words "death" and "victory" be used in the same sentence? While Satan does "sting" us through death, he does not have the final word. God has given us ultimate victory through Jesus Christ. The promise of the empty tomb is that we, too, will be raised.

While Satan does "sting" us through death, he does not have the final word.

A good friend of mine, Chris Gubelman, lived many difficult years with cystic fibrosis. Chris was a potter by trade and a very creative man. During his last days, he wrote a beautiful song expressing his faith in life after death. I share his song below:

Remember when you come to weep
At the place where my body sleeps,
I'm not lying beneath this stone.
I stand on a rock. I've gone home.
I stand on the rock of Jesus. I've gone home.

From plain old dust and common red clay,
On the rock of Jesus I stand today.
By his love I've flown away.
I've gone home. I've gone home.

Master potter, rock of my soul,
Forged me in pain and made me whole.
You helped me stand upon your rock.
You taught me to hold, to rise, and walk.

I'm not red clay beneath this marker stone;
I'm a fine clay vessel in the master's home.
From common red clay and dust and bone.
I've gone home. I've gone home.

With trials he pushed me higher,
Forging endurance in his cleansing fire.
From common red clay and dust and bone,
Reborn as porcelain, at last, I'm home.

Death, oh Death, where is your sting?
My Jesus has changed everything.
Unwrapped Lazarus and set him free.
At last those words were said to me.

Master potter, rock of my soul,
Forged me in pain and made me whole.
You helped me stand upon your rock.
You taught me to hold, to rise, and walk.
Just common red clay and dust and bone
Transformed by grace, I'm finally home.

Chris' eyes were on his heavenly home. He understood God's ultimate purpose for him and well knew God's assurances of life after death. Absorb the comfort and peace of the passages below. Read them as if for the first time.

Keep yourselves in God's love as you wait for the mercy of our Lord Jesus Christ to bring you to *eternal life.* (Jude 1:21)

I tell you the truth, whoever hears my word and believes him who sent me has *eternal life* and will not be condemned; he has crossed over from death to life. (John 5:24)

To those who by persistence in doing good seek glory, honor and immortality, he will give *eternal life.* (Rom. 2:7)

I give them *eternal life,* and they shall never perish; no one can snatch them out of my hand. (John 10:28)

Death is not the end for our loved ones in Christ, and sorrow and pain do not destroy our hope.

Death is not the end for our loved ones in Christ, and sorrow and pain do not destroy our hope. We have assurances—from God himself—of life everlasting with him. Paul provided these words of hope for the Thessalonians, and they provide hope for us too:

> We do not want you to be ignorant about those who fall asleep, or to grieve like the rest of men, who have no hope. We believe that Jesus died and rose again and so

we believe that God will bring with Jesus those who have fallen asleep in him. (1 Thess. 4:13–14)

The empty tomb was the answer to their despair, and it is the answer to ours. The familiar saying, "We don't always know what the future holds, but we know who holds the future," is one we can live by.

New life on earth can be yours.

As wonderful as the hope of heaven is, that is not the only hope we have—we also have assurances of abundant life on the earth. David, in spite of all his sorrow, made this confident assertion:

I am confident of this: I will see the goodness of the Lord *in the land of the living.* (Ps. 27:13)

God's goodness is not reserved only for heaven; we can be confident that it is available to us *now*—in the "land of the living."

It's amazing how many references to *life* there are in the four Gospels. Jesus talked much about life—his life, our lives, future life, the right kind of life, eternal life, full life, new life, lost life, and found life. And he spoke of this life as something we have *now.*

We sometimes make the mistake of thinking that "eternal life" begins when we get to heaven; but eternal life begins here on earth. Note the present tense in the following verse.

I tell you the truth, whoever hears my word and believes him who sent me *has* eternal life and will not be condemned; he *has* crossed over from death to life. (John 5:24)

Jesus is the Life-Giver, and he came to earth that we could have life—not just any life, not just a life of mediocrity—but a full life.

I have come that they may have life, and have it to the *full.* (John 10:10)

As a Christian, you have living in you the Spirit of God, and when you relinquish control of your life to him, you will learn what it means to have life "to the full." Note that this life is possible because of the *empty tomb.*

If the Spirit of him *who raised Jesus from the dead* is living in you, he who raised Christ from the dead will also give life to your mortal bodies through his Spirit, who lives in you. (Rom. 8:10–11)

The death of my wife, Claudette, taught me much about *life.* Although I will always miss her and life will never be the same without her, I have found a new life for myself. I want to share with you a few of the lessons I learned after passing through the storm of her death.

1. I learned that things could always be worse. I don't care what your situation is, you don't have to look very far before you find someone who's in a situation far worse.

2. I learned the importance of family—both physical and spiritual. I learned to value my sister-in-law, Flo, during the dark hours of Claudette's last few days. She was there with me, and she encouraged me and kept me going. But it wasn't only my physical family that kept me going, my spiritual family kept me going as well. One couple in particular, Stan and Debbie Webb, held me up when I couldn't stand on my own. They gave me a great gift: they allowed me to say whatever I wanted to say in their presence, without any inhibitions. If I had a need, a struggle, a problem, I could confess it to them and they wouldn't think any less of me. They said, "We're going to walk with you through this storm," and they did.

3. I learned that the amount of joy we are capable of experiencing is in direct proportion to the amount of pain we experience. I know that sounds strange, but it's true. When life puts you on the floor, when it completely devastates you, if you can learn and grow through that pain, you will find beyond the storm a joy far greater than you've ever experienced before. I now have a deeper level of joy, a greater passion for life, because I know what pain is.

The amount of joy we are capable of experiencing is in direct proportion to the amount of pain we experience.

4. I learned the importance of being honest with my emotions. The psalms written by David exude honesty. David expressed his fears, his anger, his impatience, his doubts—David was honest with his emotions, and we can be too.

5. I learned to live one day at a time. That's in the Bible, you know: "Do not worry about tomorrow, for tomorrow will worry about itself. Each day has enough trouble of its own" (Matt. 6:34). Claudette and I tried to life one day at a time.

6. I learned to say and do it today. Don't wait until tomorrow to tell someone you love them or to share special times together. You may not have tomorrow. Claudette and I had a nighttime routine that allowed us to spend quality time together each day. I would climb up in Claudette's bed; I'd rub her back, and we'd read Scripture and sing songs. My memories of those times are very comforting to me now.

7. I learned that Jesus went to the Cross, and he didn't want to go either.

8. I learned to trust when there is no answer. I believe there are some things in life that we'll *never* understand. We're going to have to walk by faith and not by sight.

9. I learned that there are two nonnegotiables in life: Jesus is Lord, and the Bible is the Word of God. Live by these truths.

10. I learned the importance of being content with what I have and where I am. Somewhere along the way, I picked up this little definition of happiness, and it has meant a lot to me: "Happiness is not having what you want but wanting what you have."

11. I learned to be realistic. Sometimes we just have to accept that this is what is going to happen and then go on. There are some things we just cannot change.

12. I learned the grace of receiving. I try to be a giving person, but I found out a long time ago that sometimes I have to sit down and allow people to give to me.

There is life beyond the storm. The foundation of this life is Christ and him alone, and the validation of that new life is the empty tomb.

You have the power to overcome.

The empty tomb of our Savior is proof of God's power. If God was able to overcome death and raise Jesus from the dead, he can surely bring us through the storms of our lives.

Paul makes an amazing assertion in the book of Ephesians. His prayer for their "enlightenment" is for us too:

> I pray also that the eyes of your heart may be enlightened in order that you may know . . . his incomparably great power for us who believe. That power *is like the working of his mighty strength, which he exerted in Christ when he raised him from the dead* and seated him at his right hand in the heavenly realms. (Eph. 1:18–20)

Talk about power! The same power that raised Jesus from the dead is available to us in our lives. Is there anything we cannot overcome with this power in our lives?

Too many Christians go through life not tapping into this amazing power. It's like living in the dark when we could have free access to light by just plugging the cord into the outlet. We, too, may need the "eyes of our hearts" enlightened.

Romans 8 is a favorite of storm survivors and for good reason. Here, Paul asks four questions and answers each one. These answers give us courage and assurance that, with God, we *can* overcome.

> 1. *If God is for us, who can be against us?*
> Answer: No one. Since God did not spare even his own Son, we can be assured that he will graciously give us all things.

2. *Who will bring any charge against those whom God has chosen?*
   Answer: No one. It is God who justifies.
3. *Who is he that condemns?*
   Answer: No one. The raised Christ intercedes for us.
4. *Who shall separate us from the love of Christ?*
   Answer: No one and no thing! (Rom. 8:31–39)

What confidence we have as God's children! God is in control, and he will take care of his own. Paul ended chapter eight with one of the greatest statements of confidence found in Scripture.

> In all these things we are more than conquerors through him who loved us. For I am convinced that neither death nor life, neither angels nor demons, neither the present nor the future, nor any powers, neither height nor depth, nor anything else in all creation, will be able to separate us from the love of God that is in Christ Jesus our Lord. (Rom. 8:37–39)

The same power that emptied the tomb lives in us today.

The empty tomb was the greatest miracle of all time. Our trust is not unfounded, for we trust in the God of the impossible. While Satan will continue to send storms into the lives of God's children, we know that we have the power to overcome because the same power that emptied the tomb lives in us today.

Nothing has ever proven too difficult for God; he will never disappoint us.

As the waves of trouble beat upon the shores of your life, God stands ready to empty the tomb again if he has to. He won't leave you to fight alone. You might not be able to stop the waves, but you can "learn to surf" with God's help. The empty tomb remains a monument of hope as we pass through troubled waters.

CHAPTER 8

Assurances from **God's Word**

Why Must We Suffer?

Sufferers from the beginning of time have asked "Why?" "Why must I suffer?" "Is it God's will that I suffer?" These are big questions, and the answers we come up with are incomplete at best. But the Bible does offer insight into the question of suffering.

Let's begin with an even more fundamental question: Is it okay to question God?

It's okay to question God.

Just a quick look at some Old Testament figures lets us know that God accepts our questions.

The book of Judges contains a classic story about one who questioned God. The Midianites were oppressing God's people, and when they cried to God for help, God sent an angel to Gideon in response.

> When the angel of the Lord appeared to Gideon, he said, "The Lord is with you, mighty warrior."
>
> "But sir," Gideon replied, "if the Lord is with us, *why has all this happened to us?* Where are all his wonders that our fathers told us about when they said, 'Did not the Lord bring us up out of Egypt?' But now the Lord has abandoned us and put us into the hand of Midian." (Judg. 6:12–13)

Gideon had heard the Exodus stories of God's amazing power as a child, but he wanted to know what God was doing *now!* The Lord responded:

> "Go in the strength you have and save Israel out of Midian's hand. Am I not sending you?"
>
> "But Lord," Gideon asked, "how can I save Israel? My clan is the weakest in Manasseh, and I am the least in my family."
>
> The Lord answered, *"I will be with you,* and you will strike down all the Midianites as if they were but one man." (Judg. 6:14–16)

Gideon's story shows that questioning God doesn't indicate a lack of faith; rather, it can be a stepping stone to a greater faith.

Abraham is another example of one who questioned God. When it became evident to Abraham that God intended to destroy Sodom and Gomorrah, Abraham raised a host of questions. We're amazed at Abraham's boldness.

Questioning God can be a stepping stone to a greater faith.

> Will you sweep away the righteous with the wicked? What if there are fifty righteous people in the city? Will you really sweep it away and not spare the place for the sake of the fifty righteous people in it? Far be it from you to do such a thing—to kill the righteous with the wicked, treating the righteous and the wicked alike. Far be it from you! Will not the Judge of all the earth do right? (Gen. 18:23–25)

How dare a man question God in this manner? But God was patient with Abraham's questioning and eventually agreed to save the cities if only ten righteous people could be found. What a loving God we have who allows mere mortals to question him—and even allows himself to be swayed by them.

This wasn't the first time Abraham had asked God some serious questions. God had promised Abraham that he would make a great nation out of him (Gen. 12:2–3). But as Abraham and Sarah got older and still had no children, Abraham began to doubt the promise.

You have given me no children; so a servant in my household will be my heir. (Gen. 15:2–3)

But God doesn't make promises lightly, and he never fails to fulfill them.

[God] took him outside and said, "Look up at the heavens and count the stars—if indeed you can count them." Then he said to him, "So shall your offspring be." (Gen. 15:5)

What a loving God we have who allows mere mortals to question him.

God did not chastise Abraham for his questioning, but allowed it; Abraham's questions brought him to a greater faith in God.

Moses also questioned God's actions. His boldness, like Abraham's, is surprising:

Moses heard the people of every family wailing, each at the entrance to his tent. The Lord became exceedingly angry, and Moses was troubled. He asked the Lord, "Why have you brought this trouble on your servant? What have I done to displease you that you put the burden of all these people on me? Did I conceive all these people? Did I give them birth? Why do you tell me to carry them in my arms, as a nurse carries an infant, to the land you promised on oath to their forefathers? Where can I get meat for all these people? They keep wailing to me, 'Give us meat to eat!' I cannot carry all these people by myself; the burden is too heavy for me. If this is how you are going to treat me, put me to death right now—if I have found favor in your eyes—and do not let me face my own ruin." (Num. 11:10–15)

Moses was at the end of his rope. He had seen God act in the past, but he was confused as to why God wasn't acting now! In fact, he was so discouraged that he said, "If this is how you are going to treat me, put me to death right now." Do you ever feel like Moses felt? Does the burden of pain seem too great to bear, to the point that you simply want to escape it all?

God allowed Moses to express his doubts and frustrations, and then he responded by putting the Spirit that was on Moses on seventy other men as well, so they could help Moses carry the burden of the people.

The interaction between God and Moses was healthy, even though some serious questions were asked. The questions were a natural response to a troubling situation. Asking questions of God didn't keep Gideon, Abraham, or Moses from being counted as great examples of faith (Heb. 11:8–10, 24–28, 32).

When you find yourself questioning God, you can know that you are in good company. But use your questions as a means to a greater faith; don't allow them to fester and turn into bitterness and doubt. If you need help finding answers, read the stories of the storm survivors in this book or go to someone you know who has experienced a similar storm and has emerged victorious.

God is not offended by your questions. He answers them with assurances of his neverfailing presence, his ever-present concern, and the promise of the empty tomb. He *will* bring you through your storm.

God is not the source of your pain.

When the storms come, many look up and ask, "Did God send the storm?"

Job's wife, in the Old Testament book of Job, was so sure that God was the source of Job's suffering that she suggested that Job "curse God and die" (Job 2:9).

Many respond to the death of a loved one by saying that God took their loved one. Others, in the face of tragedy, say that it was God's will. Some insurance policies even refer to tornadoes, hurricanes, and earthquakes as "acts of God." However, the book of Job makes it clear that Satan was the one who created the problems for Job. In the first two chapters of Job, we are privy to a conversation between God and Satan.

> Then the Lord said to Satan, "Have you considered my servant Job? There is no one on earth like him; he is blameless and upright, a man who fears God and shuns evil. And he still maintains his integrity, though you incited me against him to ruin him without any reason."
>
> "Skin for skin!" Satan replied. "A man will give all he has for his own life. But stretch out your hand and strike his flesh and bones, and he will surely curse you to your face."
>
> The Lord said to Satan, "Very well, then, he is in your hands; but you must spare his life."
>
> So Satan went out from the presence of the Lord and afflicted Job with painful sores from the soles of his feet

to the top of his head. Then Job took a piece of broken pottery and scraped himself with it as he sat among the ashes. (Job 2:3–8)

Even though Job didn't know about the conversation between Satan and God, he wasn't willing to blame God for his trouble.

In all this, Job did not sin by charging God with wrong-doing. (Job 1:22)

But we can see behind the scenes, and we can see that the source of Job's storm was Satan. He is the source of your storm too!

Paul confirmed that the source of our suffering is Satan when he referred to his thorn in the flesh as a "messenger of Satan" (2 Cor. 12:7). Jesus also connected suffering with Satan. When the synagogue ruler criticized Jesus for healing a woman on the Sabbath, Jesus said,

You hypocrites! Doesn't each of you on the Sabbath untie his ox or donkey from the stall and lead it out to give it water? Then should not this woman, a daughter of Abraham, *whom Satan has kept bound* for eighteen long years, be set free on the Sabbath day from what bound her? (Luke 13:15–16)

Satan is the author of suffering, sickness, pain, and death—he is the author of all that is evil. In talking about the significance of Jesus' death, the Hebrew writer tells us that Jesus died so "he might destroy him *who holds the power of death*—that is, the devil" (Heb. 2:14).

James tells us that all temptations come from Satan:

> When tempted, no one should say, "God is tempting me." For God cannot be tempted by evil, nor does he tempt anyone. (James 1:13)

James goes on to affirm that God is the author of good, not evil:

> Every good and perfect gift is from above, coming down from the Father of the heavenly lights, who does not change like shifting shadows. (James 1:17)

While the ultimate source of our suffering is Satan, the wrong choices of ourselves and others often contribute to our pain. We can receive forgiveness for wrong choices, but not all of the consequences can be removed. The law of sowing and reaping proclaims,

> Do not be deceived: God cannot be mocked. A man reaps what he sows. (Gal. 6:7)

Adam and Eve chose to listen to the wrong voice—Satan—and they suffered the consequences: pain in childbearing for the woman and painful toil for the man (Gen. 3:16–19).

Satan is the author of suffering, sickness, pain, and death—he is the author of all that is evil.

The bad choices of others also bring pain into our lives. World leaders, such as Hitler, make choices that affect the lives of millions. The date of April 19, 1995 will stand forever etched in the minds of many people in Oklahoma. Someone chose to blow up the federal building in Oklahoma City and many lost their lives. The man who chooses to drive drunk may kill the loved one of another. The woman who chooses to have an affair with a married man may disrupt an innocent woman's marriage.

Because Satan has power in this world, storms will come. But God never abandons us; in fact, he takes the evil that Satan sends and finds ways to bring blessings out of pain.

There are blessings in pain.

As difficult as it is to see anything good in the midst of a storm, there are blessings to be found in the worst of circumstances. Romans 8 assures us that "in all things God works for the good of those who love him" (Rom. 8:28). Let's look at some of the blessings of pain.

Suffering matures us.

> Consider it pure joy, my brothers, whenever you face trials of many kinds, because you know that the testing of your faith develops perseverance. Perseverance must finish its work so that you may be mature and complete, not lacking anything. (James 1:2–4)

David understood the maturing benefits of struggle:

> It was good for me to be afflicted so that I might learn your decrees. (Ps. 119:71)

Suffering teaches us to be grateful. When someone has endured intense pain, pain-free days are fantastic and days of only mild pain are appreciated. It doesn't take much to make those who have experienced intense pain grateful. The degree of happiness you experience in life is in direct proportion to the amount of pain you have experienced.

Our suffering can benefit others. Paul declared God to be the God of comfort,

> who comforts us in all our troubles, so that we can comfort those in any trouble with the comfort we ourselves have received from God. (2 Cor. 1:3–4)

The comfort you receive in your suffering allows you to reach out and touch others. Paul declared that shared suffering allows for shared comfort.

> For just as the sufferings of Christ flow over into our lives, so also through Christ our comfort overflows. If we are distressed, it is for your comfort and salvation; if we are comforted, it is for your comfort, which produces in you patient endurance of the same sufferings we suffer. And our hope for you is firm, because we know that just as you share in our sufferings, so also you share in our comfort. (2 Cor. 1:5–7)

When you are experiencing problems in a certain area, you don't look for someone who has read a book on the subject—you look for someone who has experienced the same type of problem. I am better equipped to help others who face the loss of a terminally ill loved one because I lived through my wife's five-year fight with cancer. I didn't seek out this experience, but sharing the lessons I learned is a natural response.

Suffering teaches us to rely on God. As Paul looked back on his sufferings, he saw a definite spiritual benefit.

> We do not want you to be uninformed, brothers, about the hardships we suffered in the province of Asia. We were under great pressure, far beyond our ability to endure, so that we despaired even of life. Indeed, in our hearts we felt the sentence of death. But this happened that we *might not rely on ourselves but on God,* who raises the dead. He has delivered us from such a deadly peril, and he will deliver us. On him we have set our hope that he will continue to deliver us. (2 Cor. 1:8–10)

Paul described himself as being under "great pressure." He said that he "despaired even of life." But he saw a benefit in his suffering—he learned to rely on God.

The comfort you receive in your suffering allows you to reach out and touch others.

Suffering brings us into a closer union with Christ. The goal for all of Jesus' disciples is to be like him. Being like Jesus includes participating in his sufferings. Paul said,

> I want to know Christ and the power of his resurrection and the fellowship of sharing in his sufferings, becoming like him in his death, and so, somehow, to attain to the resurrection from the dead. (Phil. 3:10–11)

Paul saw the value in sufferings as it related to Christ-likeness. How can Christians say they really know Christ when suffering has never been a part of their lives? Peter also connected suffering with following the example of Jesus.

> To this you were called, because Christ suffered for you, leaving you an example, that you should follow in his steps. . . .
> When they hurled their insults at him, he did not retaliate; when he suffered, he made no threats. Instead, he entrusted himself to him who judges justly. (1 Pet. 2:21–23)

Jesus didn't deserve to suffer—his suffering resulted from the wrong choices of others. When we feel that the storms we are called to endure are unfair and undeserved, we can look to Jesus as the ultimate example of unjust suffering and thus gain strength to go on.

How can we say we really know Christ when suffering has never been a part of our lives?

Life's sufferings can either be a stepping stone or a stumbling block. Suffering is not something we choose, nor something God chooses for us, but when Satan works harm in our lives, we can thwart his efforts by claiming the blessings of pain.

You can adopt a new view of suffering.

Storms are never pleasant—their nature is to unsettle, destroy, confuse, and wreck havoc. Yet part of our ability to endure these inevitable storms is in our outlook. The apostle Paul can teach us much about suffering; we learn from him a new view.

Suffering is not impossible to endure. The severity of the dangers Paul encountered is unbelievable (see 2 Cor. 11:24 ff); yet even in expressing the pressures he felt, he consistently maintained that they were not unbearable:

> We are hard pressed on every side, *but not crushed;* perplexed, *but not in despair;* persecuted, *but not abandoned;* struck down, *but not destroyed.* (2 Cor. 4:8–9)

By claiming that storms are not impossible to endure, I in no way am minimizing the severity of the storm or the destruction that it brings. Yet we have a promise from God that he will not give us more than we can bear and that he will always provide a way out *so that we can stand up under it.*

> No temptation has seized you except what is common to man. And God is faithful; he will not let you be tempted beyond what you can bear. But when you are tempted, he will also provide a way out so that you can stand up under it. (1 Cor. 10:13)

Suffering is momentary. Paul was able to view suffering as momentary because he saw it as part of a larger picture. He knew that the important part of the picture is in the realm of the unseen; and this is where he tells us to fix our eyes.

223

Therefore we do not lost heart. Though outwardly we are wasting away, yet inwardly we are being renewed day by day. For our light and *momentary* troubles are achieving for us an eternal glory that far outweighs them all. So we fix our eyes not on what is seen, but on what is unseen. For what is seen is temporary, but what is unseen is eternal. (2 Cor. 4:16–18)

"He will not let you be tempted beyond what you can bear."

Suffering brings our future reward into clear view. Abraham was able to endure difficulty because he was "looking forward to the city with foundations, whose architect and builder is God" (Heb. 11:10). Moses was able to endure mistreatment because he looked ahead to his reward with eyes of faith.

By faith Moses . . . regarded disgrace for the sake of Christ as of greater value than the treasures of Egypt, because he was looking ahead to his reward. (Heb. 11:24–26)

Paul, too, knew this world wasn't his home and was able to look ahead to his future reward.

Now we know that if the earthly tent we live in is destroyed, we have a building from God, an eternal house in heaven, not built by human hands. Meanwhile we groan, longing to be clothed with our heavenly dwelling, because when we are clothed, we will not be found naked. For while we are in this tent, we groan and are burdened, because we do not wish to be unclothed but to be clothed with our heavenly dwelling, so that what is mortal may be swallowed up by life. Now it is God who has made us for this very purpose and has given us the Spirit as a deposit, guaranteeing what is to come. (2 Cor. 5:1–5)

Suffering must be viewed through eyes of trust. Trusting God when we can't see his hand or hear his voice requires all the faith we can muster. You may identify with the pain and frustration in the following words from David. Notice his concluding thoughts.

> How long, O Lord? Will you forget me forever?
>   How long will you hide your face from me?
> How long must I wrestle with my thoughts
>   and every day have sorrow in my heart?
>   How long will my enemy triumph over me?
> Look on me and answer, O Lord my God.
>   Give light to my eyes, or I will sleep in death;
> my enemy will say, "I have overcome him,"
>   and my foes will rejoice when I fall.
> But *I trust in your unfailing love;*
>   my heart rejoices in your salvation.
> I will sing to the Lord,
>   *for he has been good to me.*
>   (Ps. 13)

In all that David went through, he continued to trust in God and to proclaim his goodness. He looked beyond the present and trusted God to keep his promises.

Anytime we can look back on a storm, we see it with clearer vision than while we're in the midst of it. When Job was able to see his sufferings from the other side of pain, he realized that God had been in control all along and that it was he who lacked understanding. At the end of the story, we see a man whose faith is still intact and more real and genuine than ever. When he finally saw God's greatness and majesty, he responded with awe-filled respect and appreciation.

> Then Job replied to the Lord:
> "I know that you can do all things;
>   no plan of yours can be thwarted. . . .
>   Surely I spoke of things I did not understand,
>   things too wonderful for me to know. . . .
> My ears had heard of you
>   but now my eyes have seen you."
> (Job 42:1–3, 5–6)

God is there whether we can see his hand or not. Suffering is a natural part of this dark world, but God has sent the light of his Son into our darkness to guide us through the storm and into his eternal light.